Goodness a...

All the days of my life

A Memoir

'Your statutes have been my songs
In the house of my pilgrimage.

Your promise is well tried,
And your servant loves it.'

Psalm 119 vv. 54 and 140

Published for Wilma Nicolson by Verité CM Ltd.

ISBN No: 978-1-914388-48-4

Typesetting and photographs by Cherrie Irwin

Printed by
Verité CM Ltd, Worthing, West Sussex BN12 4BG UK.

www.veritecm.com

Acknowledgments

There will be some reading this book who have travelled a major part of this journey with me. To them I want to give heartfelt thanks for a lifetime of love, support and friendship. Among them is Jim Dainty. His wife Angela was another fellow pupil midwife and together they have supported me from afar through many ups and downs. I have used Jim's unsolicited commendation as foreword for this book.

Each and every friendship, whether from those early years or made in much more recent days is very precious and hugely valued. I thank God for you.

Thank you to those who read this material at an earlier stage and encouraged me to proceed to publication. Particular thanks go to Cherrie Irwin whose willing help at every stage of this project, but especially in these final days of preparation, has been invaluable. While the story is mine, the presentation of the book as you have it in your hand today is largely due to her many hours of work. Thank you, Cherrie.

I am indebted to Chris Powell and his team at Verite CM Ltd for their friendly helpfulness, guidance and professionalism – all much appreciated.

All Scripture quotations are from the Revised Standard Version (RSV) except where otherwise stated.

Foreword

In Psalm 39, King David writes - *I am Your passing guest, a temporary resident, as all my fathers were.*

David uses a dynamic picture of God, from his experience and culture. In Jewish culture, it was an honour and a duty to provide for any traveller in need of hospitality. David says that God treats us as passing guests in this world and while we are here, he accepts responsibility for us. He will make provision for us and provide protection for us – if we are willing to trust him.

Wilma writes of her 80 years as a temporary resident in this world. In these years there have been adventure and joys. But also times of trial and disappointment. Her testimony is clear – in every situation God has treated her as a beloved child and guest for whom he accepted responsibility.

I have been spiritually nourished in reading this memoir and warmly commend it to you. May you too discover the goodness and mercy of God in all the days of your life.

Rev. Dr James E. Dainty

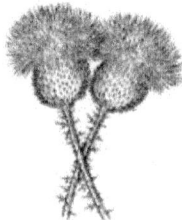

Contents

Contents

Prologue

You would have found it on the back road in Helmsdale, a little single story building clad in red corrugated iron, the Free Presbyterian church long since transformed into a comfortable dwelling house. The few worshippers always streamed out the moment the officiating elder pronounced the benediction. As I walked out amongst them, one Sunday in the summer of 1965, the words of John 11:40 were burning themselves into my heart and mind. In the wording of the old King James Version (KJV), the only Bible version in common use at the time, 'Said I not unto thee that if thou wouldst believe thou shouldst see the glory of God?'. Presumably the story of the raising of Lazarus had been the focus of the sermon that day, nothing else of what was said has remained with me, only those words spoken to Martha by Jesus. I was very much a baby Christian at the time. I have never again read the story of the raising of Lazarus, without recalling that scene of nearly 60 years ago. How much of His glory God has revealed to me since then!

How does God reveal His glory? And how has He revealed it to me? Now that gave me occasion for a lot of reflection as I set about writing this memoir, since its prime purpose is to bring glory to Him.

Of course God reveals His glory in His creation. He has placed me in beautiful places – Scotland being amongst the foremost!

Even if youth and familiarity prevented my appreciating it in early life as I was growing up, my memory brings scenes to mind which cause me to worship God in retrospect. I think of the hour or two I spent sitting on a grassy slope surrounded by thick yellow gorse bushes, just beyond my dear friend Janet's home at Carnlaggie, on the outskirts of the village and the end of the golf course, at the foot of the Helmsdale river. It was a warm summer's Sunday afternoon. My sister Jean and family were home on holiday. I had made lunch for us all and now that it was cleared up, they had gone to visit the Traill grandparents, and my Mum and Dad had gone for a run in the car. I was revelling in the solitude and silence apart from the hum of the occasional passing car on the road below. In front of me was the familiar and much-loved view 'up the Strath'. The heather-clad hills rising steeply on either side of the flat valley bottom with its fields of hay or corn stooks, flowering potatoes, flocks of sheep and a few cows. I could see the narrow single-track road winding down one side of the lazy river and the railway line the other.

In my hands on my lap was my Bible, and I was reading in 2 Chronicles chapters 5 and 6, the dedication of Solomon's temple. We read there how 'the house of the Lord was filled with a cloud so that the priests could not stand to minister because of the cloud; for the glory of the Lord filled the house of God'. Scripture goes on to quote Solomon's wonderful prayer of dedication which includes: 'O LORD, God of Israel, there is no God like you, in heaven or on earth, keeping covenant and showing steadfast love to your servants who walk before you with all their heart...'. God certainly revealed His glory to me that day, not only in the beauty of His creation but in His living Word, the Bible, causing me to worship Him with all my heart.

God's glory can also be revealed in people He has created – I praise Him for the Godly saints who have crossed my path over the years but are now with Christ and with whom I eagerly look forward to spending eternity in God's nearer presence.

There is yet another way by which God reveals His glory. In Exodus 33:18 we read of Moses asking God 'Show me your glory...'. God answered, 'I will make all my goodness pass before you, and will proclaim to you my name...'. And that is just how He has shown me His glory continually throughout all of life – by showering me with His goodness and in so doing revealing to me His name – that name which is above all other names.

It is my prayer that God's glory may be revealed to the reader of this book as I share with you how His goodness and mercy *have* followed me all the days of my life.

God revealed Himself initially to Moses in Exodus 3:14 as 'I AM', the self-existent, ever living One. Jesus Christ who is one with His Father is described in Hebrews 13:8 as 'the same yesterday, today and forever'. How precious that is to know in this constantly changing world! Many years ago I came across and recorded in my *'little black book'* (which I used for such things), a quote of the Puritan Thomas Hogg: 'The unchangeableness of my God is my rock'. That truth has certainly been a rock for me down through the years!

We read of other names of God, such as 'Jehovah Jireh', the God who provides, 'El-Roi', the God who sees, or 'Jehovah Shammah', the Lord is my companion. I hope to show how God has been all of these to me and more since He first revealed Himself to me as my Saviour and Redeemer 60 years ago.

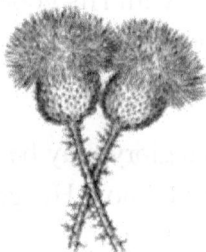

Chapter 1

Early Days

The youngest of three children, I was born on my brother's fourth birthday in the county of Sutherland in the far north of Scotland. My sister arrived one year and thirteen days after my brother, while I came along just thirteen days short of three years behind her! Being so close in age, my brother and sister were always great playmates but often had to tolerate allowing little sister to tag along. They both grew very tall, while I remained forever very short. They were both fair skinned and had green eyes while I was born with jet black hair and blue eyes. All of that seemed to set the scene for the different path God had planned for me.

When I was ten years old we moved into the home of my paternal grandmother which was in fact her family home. She had been living in County Durham with her husband and two little boys when sadly in 1918, her husband died in the dreadful 'Spanish flu' pandemic. The boys were three and four years old. Their mother brought them back to her family home near the village of Helmsdale on Scotland's north east coast, where her bachelor brother helped her bring them up. Both Granny and her brother were still alive when we moved in with them some thirty-five years later.

My father was a stone mason and bricklayer by trade though he could 'turn his hand to anything' to use a common expression. He set about modernizing the substantial stone house which his grandfather had built in 1901, creating from the horse's stable a kitchen with electricity and running water and a bathroom from the tiny scullery behind. Being the elder of the two boys he had to leave school early to support the family, but he had the potential for so much more than the trade he followed. In later years, he taught bricklaying at the local Technical College and drew up the plans for many a local building or home extension.

'Religion' didn't figure largely in our home – yet it did! Many were the bitter rows, my parents' upbringing having been on either side of a denominational divide, while Granny held tenaciously (and legalistically, it has to be said), to hers. To avoid upsetting Granny, there were many things we were not allowed to do on Sunday. Before my father got a car, we frequently walked the two miles to church in Helmsdale and two miles home again. Then back for the evening service at Communion time. Communion was celebrated three times a year in Presbyterian circles. The Communion service was three hours long, and the evening service two hours. One of the three Communion services was held annually in June, and it always seemed to fall on a hot summer's day!

My mother was diagnosed with Multiple Sclerosis when I was about nine years old. By the time I was twelve she was wheelchair dependent. So on these Communion Sundays my sister and I had to do the meal for us all when we got home from church after 3 pm, then wash up before setting off for the two mile walk back to church for the evening service.

Granny's and Dad's minister would visit every few weeks on a Sunday so the television in our family room had to be summarily switched off, and the Sunday papers hastily stuffed behind cushions on his arrival. It was something that was never discussed seriously as a family nor commented on between us siblings, but it was something I found so inconsistent, even hypocritical. The family strife stirred up by 'church' was something I knew I would not miss when the time came to leave home. Strangely however, rather than wanting nothing more to do with church, I found myself looking forward to finding one I could enjoy going to.

Our family always had strong links with Glasgow through relatives of Dad's. Then those ties were strengthened when both my brother and sister left home to go there, my brother apprenticed to one of the large ship-building companies while my sister went to teacher training college. My breaking the mould by going to Aberdeen was not too popular! The family of the school friend with whom I was going to do nurse training had friends in Aberdeen who would 'keep an eye' on us. Also, the boy I had been going out with for several years was in university there – so it was to Aberdeen I went.

In those days of 'apprenticeship' nurse training – before it became a university degree course – we had every weekend off for the first three months. Most of the girls were 'local' enough to go home at weekends, but not Doris and me. After joining them at church on Sunday morning, Doris' family's friends, or other church members, took us home for lunch each week. While we waited for our hosts, I observed how happily everyone stood around chatting, seeming to be in no hurry to leave – a very sharp contrast to my experience of church in the little red building on the back road in Helmsdale! Over lunch we invariably discussed what we had heard at church, it all seemed so natural to them, again a sharp contrast to my experience at home where on arrival our Bibles were wordlessly returned to the shelf.

As time went on, what I was hearing began to sink in. The familiar message I had heard from childhood – that I was a sinner – hadn't changed, but it became so much clearer to me that God had sent His only Son, Jesus, to take the punishment for my sins. His death on the cross satisfied God's righteous judgment, I was reconciled to Him, and I could go free! More than that, Jesus' rising again from the dead proved Himself to be who He had said He was – none other than the Son of God, now returned to His Father. Seated at His right hand, alive for evermore, He was interceding for me on a daily basis. I had an advocate with the Father – could my feeble mind fully comprehend such a wonder?

However, I am leaping ahead. I did not come to such a full understanding all at once. What I did come to see was that the life that these Christian friends were living, their evident satisfaction with God and enjoyment of each other's friendship both inside and outside of Sunday church, was the way for me to go and I set about making the changes in my life that I saw to be necessary. One of those changes was major. The boy I had been keeping company with for several years now had no interest whatever in my new-found convictions. I had brought him along to church, but he just laughed. After a few months of inner conflict on this issue, there was ultimately a sense of relief when the relationship was finally ended.

I was free now to fully live as a Christian, but it wasn't long before I came to see that I couldn't do it! I couldn't maintain the love, joy, peace, patience etc that a Christian should be exhibiting. I came to understand for the first time that my biggest problem was *myself!* Although I had given mental assent to the fact that I was a sinner, I now *knew* that I was a sinner and that I *needed* Jesus! Now the truth of Jesus' death cancelling out my sin became wonderfully and personally real. To be told that God saw me only through the perfection of His Son and that I had been clothed in the righteousness of Christ, drew from me such love and gratitude and had the effect of spurring me on to greater effort to live a life of obedience to His commands. And now was the time, too, to grasp the truth about the Holy Spirit, the third Person of the Trinity, sent by Christ at Pentecost but foretold by Him and recorded for us in John chapter 14, where Jesus described Him as the Paraclete – the One called alongside to help. So I wasn't doing this on my own, but as a believer in Jesus I was now indwelt by His Holy Spirit who would help me to overcome temptation and live according to God's will.

Now began in earnest my life in the Spirit, learning to live out in practice what I was inwardly being taught as I read the Bible for myself and taking every opportunity to hear it preached by Godly leaders.

Life would never be the same again. As I write I have just passed the 60th anniversary of being baptized as a believer.

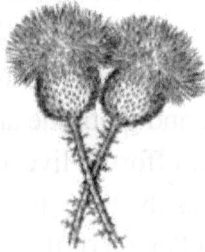

Chapter 2

Keswick

All that I have described was happening during my years as a
student nurse in Aberdeen and while I was worshipping Sunday
by Sunday in Union Grove Baptist Church. The church had
reached something of a low ebb. I was the 'first fruit' of a new
ministry, and my friend Doris and I were the nucleus of a newly
formed Young People's Group which went on to thrive and
grow. The friendships formed were rich and our fellowship
precious. We went as a group to Youth for Christ on a Saturday
evening as well as regular times together after the evening
service on Sundays.

On one memorable occasion, the speaker at the evening service
was a man called Charles Stern who spoke on Mary breaking
the alabaster jar and anointing Jesus with the expensive perfume
it held. He challenged his hearers to 'break the box for Jesus'.
As young people we were indeed challenged. Our planned
programme for the evening was abandoned and we spent our
time after the service on our knees in worship and prayer.

The summer of 1963 was very special. I was to sit my final
exams in the autumn, so my time in Aberdeen was coming to an
end. In June six young ladies, all students of the WEC College
in Glasgow, came to conduct a series of evangelistic meetings
based at our church. WEC was the missionary organisation

known at that time as Worldwide Evangelisation Crusade, founded by C.T. Studd in the early 20th Century. In 1982 the name became WEC International. In this name WEC stands for 'Worldwide Evangelisation for Christ'. The organisation has been a 'faith mission' since its inception, so called because each missionary serving God under its banner has to find their own support and trust God alone to meet their financial needs. Encountering WEC and its faith principle for the first time as a very new Christian, I was intrigued and challenged. I little knew then how much that challenge was to become a personal one in later life!

The WEC girls 'camped out' in the church building and church members entertained them for evening meals. During these final months of training three fellow students and myself were sharing a little flat and we had the girls for tea, three at a time. Such was the richness of the conversation around the table that I found my heart 'burn within me' as did the hearts of the two on the road to Emmaus as they walked unwittingly in the company of the risen Jesus. That story is told in Luke's gospel account, chapter 24.

Another very special experience that summer was my first visit to the Keswick Convention, in England's beautiful Lake District. I went as part of a mixed age group of people from Aberdeen brought together by Mr and Mrs Swanson – I doubt if I ever knew their first names! Mr Swanson was a retired minister to deaf people and he and his wife were a dear Godly couple who regularly hosted a house party in Keswick each year. They took me there in their car and an abiding memory is of arriving in Keswick on the first day, as thousands of others were doing. As we drove through the little town towards the Guest House, we were inching our way forward through the crowded streets. The car windows were open, and our driver was greeting smiling faces on all sides – there was that Christian family feeling that I had been introduced to on my arrival in the little Church in Aberdeen those three years before. The first meeting of the Convention was that same Saturday evening. I came from a little congregation of perhaps two hundred gathering on a Sunday and less than a dozen young people in our Young People's Fellowship. Gatherings of a similar number were my only experience of Christian life thus far, so worshipping with five thousand others in the large tent and up to two thousand in the smaller tent where the Young People's meetings were held was a very new and wonderful experience! And just imagine the singing of those five thousand voices, simply but so effectively led by the gentle playing of the piano. It was inspiring and it was thrilling.

Though that was well-nigh sixty years ago as I write, I still remember clearly the exposition each morning of the book of Hosea given by the Rev. J.R. Miller from New Zealand. He gave me an understanding of that book that has carried me through to this day. There were two other speakers each evening which would have included the Rev. Eric Alexander and the Rev. Philip Hacking, both young men themselves at that time, who spoke to the young people at our own gatherings that year. Coming from my austere childhood experience of Sunday worship it was so new to me to hear light-hearted remarks about a 'Hacking cough' and 'Alexander's Ragtime Band' dropped in occasionally before the solid Bible teaching which I thirstily drank in!

That year began my love of the Lake District and Keswick itself, with towering fells behind and a glorious vista across Lake Derwentwater with its wooded headlands and islands, to a range of other fells on the other side. One abiding memory is the solitary time of reflection and worship on Friar's Crag and another the morning walk across the silent town to the 7 am prayer meeting where we heard seasoned missionaries pray fervently for their countries of service. This new young Christian's experience was being rapidly expanded.

Friday morning of the Convention in those days was dedicated to missionary speakers from around the world. It ended with an opportunity for those who were willing to respond to God's call to full-time missionary service to show this by standing up in their place. Just recently, nearly sixty years later, living now in Northern Ireland, I find I have a neighbour and friend who stood up at that very first missionary meeting that I attended! She and her husband went on to spend all their working lives in various parts of the world with Child Evangelism Fellowship.

The final meeting of the Convention on the Friday evening was another very special occasion. Entry into the tent was restricted until all was in place for the Communion service. Long queues of eager participants formed outside the different entrances to the big tent, and all joined in the hearty singing of favourite hymns. I wonder what the local residents made of it all? Later, as thousands representing virtually every tribe and nation ate the bread and drank the wine together, I was again impacted by the realisation of the wonder of having been brought into this worldwide family of God. And I was greatly impressed by being served by the very men under whose ministry I had sat all week and whom I held in awe. How I thanked God for their example of humility!

We sang a hymn which was new to me at the close of that Communion service. It focused on the return of the Lord Jesus. I can feel the thrill of the resounding chorus now as I think of it – 'O, Lord Jesus, how long, how long ere we shout the glad song: Christ returneth, Hallelujah, Hallelujah, amen! Hallelujah, amen'. And I also recall the thrill of the realisation that I was one of so many who were all waiting for Jesus to come again 'to receive from the world His own' and, wonder of wonders, I was now one of His own!

A few weeks after my return from Keswick, and back into the busyness of work, I came home from a late shift one evening and was kneeling in the darkness beside my bed when the clock in the church tower nearby struck midnight. Some more words from that hymn sprang to mind: 'It may be at morn, it may be at twilight, it may be perchance that the blackness of midnight will burst into light in the blaze of His glory, when Jesus returns for His own'. My heart and my mind tried to imagine what it would be like if the bedroom were suddenly to burst into light in the blaze of His glory! Now sixty years later, we are still waiting for that glorious event, but we say continually 'Even so, come Lord Jesus'! (Revelation chapter 22:20)

Author H.L. Turner (1845-1915 unconfirmed)

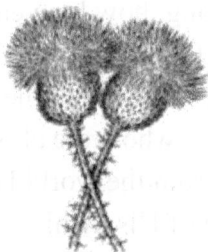

Chapter 3

'Elsie's'

Shortly after that memorable summer of 1963 I was due to sit my final exams. What then? That was the burning question. Amongst other things we had had teaching on God's guidance from our mentors at the Convention. I so needed that! I really wanted to go on to midwifery training – after all, it was the usual next step for those who had trained as Registered General Nurses (as that qualification was known in Scotland). Could I go on to do that now? My mother had Multiple Sclerosis and was confined to a wheelchair. My grandmother lived with us and was now very elderly. My sister had married and moved away. My father was working full-time. I knew that, as the single daughter, I must eventually go home to care for them all – but was this the time? I had another week's leave following the one spent at the Keswick Convention and I was going to spend it at home. On the way there I was telling God that I really needed to know *this week* what His will for my next step was to be. Places for further training needed to be booked up well in advance and my closest friends already had their plans made. I was determined to make no decision until I knew God's will for me.

At Keswick we had been advised of three things to consider when looking for God's guidance – the advice of older Christians, the circumstances and the Word of God. I had already had the advice of older Christians. These friends knew that there were no young Christians for fellowship in the village at home and no minister at that time in the church. My family did not take the Christian faith seriously. Going home as a very young Christian would not be an easy assignment and my mature Christian friends knew that. Their advice was 'Don't go if you can help it'.

On my very first evening at home the question was put to me: 'What are you going to do when you finish?' I answered by saying that perhaps I should come home to look after them all. That suggestion was met with the emphatic response that they were 'managing' and that I should go on and finish all I wanted to do. 'Thank you, Lord' I said inwardly. 'That's two of the considerations in discerning your will for me made clear, but what does your Word say?' Later that same evening I had my answer. I was at that time reading a psalm each bedtime. I had come to Psalm 45. Verses 10 and 11 read: 'Hearken, O daughter, and consider and incline your ear; forget also your own people and your father's house for so doth the king greatly desire your beauty..." I marvelled and thanked and worshipped my faithful God. In the post I received a card from one of the WEC students spoken of in the previous chapter. It remains pasted into a scrapbook of precious writings gathered and recorded over the years. On it was written: 'One step thou seest, then go forward boldly; one step is far enough for faith to see. Take that and thy next duty shall be told thee for step by step thy Lord is leading thee'.

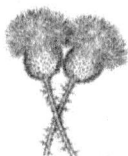

A few months later found me in Edinburgh as a pupil midwife at the Elsie Inglis Memorial Maternity Pavilion affectionately known to us as 'Elsie's'. The address of the hospital, Spring Gardens, had sounded exciting, but I was disillusioned when the taxi set me down in an area that bore no resemblance to a garden! However, the other side of the building looked directly out over Holyrood Park and time off was regularly spent walking around the Salisbury Crags or climbing Arthur's Seat – what could be better? The Royal Mile with its friendly little cafes for coffee or lunch was just a short walk away, as was a Baptist Church which I was to find provided good fellowship as well as good spiritual food.

On arrival I was asked if I was willing to share a room. I doubt if I had any option, in fact! Anyway – what sort of first impression would one make by saying 'no'? I asked who it would be with and was told it would be with the next person to come along. I silently prayed that it would either be a Christian with whom I might have fellowship or someone who God intended making His own. The latter is just what He had planned. An English girl named Joan joined me in the room. After a few months the evening came when I was preparing to go to our Nurses' Christian Fellowship (NCF) meeting and Joan asked if she could come with me. She later shared with that group how she had knelt by her bed one evening and 'asked God to do for me what He had done for Wilma'. Joan went on with the Lord and remained a dear friend until the Lord took her to her heavenly home recently at the age of eighty-three.

Elsie Inglis MMP was a very small hospital. We were eight in that particular intake of midwives and I was the only Scot – and the only one who didn't choose haggis from the menu on Robbie Burns' birthday that January! Joan was one of the two English girls. There was a girl from S. Africa and another from N. Rhodesia together with several from Ireland – not to be confused with Northern Ireland. There was one girl from that Province. Her name was Jennifer and although neither of us was aware of it at that time, God was to use Jennifer significantly in my life in future days. More on that later. Amongst the more senior pupils and those who followed us, there were several Christians and we were encouraged by a small number of Christian Staff Midwives. Apart from those mothers-to-be who for various reasons had to spend time on the antenatal ward before their babies were delivered, much more time was spent in hospital after delivery then than is the case now. We had the great joy of seeing several mothers come to faith in Christ, too!

One significant memory stands out from that time. I was due to start work in the Labour Ward. The Labour Ward Sister had quite a reputation for brooking no incompetence! We had previously been shown round at a very busy period when several babies were being delivered.

It was now the evening before I was to begin and I was scared stiff! Placing the next day in God's hands, I fell asleep only to wake up shortly after with a knot in my stomach. Why was it there, I immediately asked myself? The answer came just as swiftly – it was because I was going to work on the Labour Ward the next morning! So often that would be the end of the sleep for that night, but God would have known that I needed to be well rested. He also knew that I needed to learn to trust Him to keep His Word to His fearful child. Unbidden, the words came into my mind: 'I can do all things through Christ who gives me strength' (Philippians 4.13). Peace descended and I was asleep again in minutes.

This occurred more than once during that night. I awoke refreshed. I was so excited I just had to tell Joan what had happened, though it was before she came to faith in Jesus for herself. I went into the day greatly encouraged – and I survived! Many more days in the Labour Ward were to follow and many babies delivered. I even came to respect that Ward Sister.

It was a very happy year which passed quickly, and before I knew it I was again looking to God for direction. Was it time now to go home? Along came the night the speaker at our NCF meeting, while speaking of Philip in Acts chapter 8, said that when God asked Philip to go from the revival in Samaria to the desert for the sake of one soul, he arose and went. I knew immediately that word was for me. It was the hardest thing God has ever asked me to do.

Chapter 4

At Home

'I know…whom I have believed…and am persuaded…that He is able…to keep…that which I have committed unto Him…against that day.' (2Timothy 1:12). The rhythm of the train wheels echoed these words in my head over and over again as we sped north, away from Edinburgh and towards Helmsdale. It was early February 1965. It turned out to be a month of spring-like weather, just right for 'spring cleaning' and I redecorated the little back bedroom for my own use. My sister and brother-in-law had just had their second little boy, and Mum, Dad and I visited them for a few days in their mobile home in Caol, under the shadow of Ben Nevis. I had prepared a picnic for the journey south and Dad took us off the beaten track on the way as he loved to do. It was warm enough to have our picnic outside of the car in the beautiful surroundings of Strathglass. I'm sure those years ago and in that location we would have heard the call of the cuckoo as well as many another songbird, though my interest in birdwatching had not yet been born.

So passed the four weeks before I took up the position of Staff Nurse in the Lawson Memorial Hospital in Golspie, the village eighteen miles to the south of us and the village where I had spent the last six years of my school life. 'The Lawson' as it was affectionately known had at that time a resident consultant surgeon who was in charge of two little wards, male and female, as well as operating theatre, x-ray and outpatients departments. It was a busy little place, particularly in the summer season when the roads were busy with holiday makers. Sadly sometimes accidents happened. Such an occasion brought into the hospital none other than John Lennon of the Beatles fame and his wife Yoko Ono. That put Golspie and 'The Lawson' on the front pages for a day or two! Fortunately neither were seriously hurt.

Inexorably Mum's condition worsened and eventually I had to give up work all together and spend time at home with her. Early in my time at home Granny had taken ill and was now permanently in a place of care, her brother having died several years before. The challenges were as great as ever I had feared they would be! My father's disposition was such that made coping with the years of responsibilities at home difficult for him, and sadly he frequently spent not only a lot of time in one of the local public houses, but a lot of money, too - money which we couldn't afford. Mum could no longer look after the housekeeping and handed it all over to me. I inherited significant debt to local traders and I prayed much for the wisdom to know how to manage it all.

An evangelist came to our door one day. He asked me if I was a Christian. 'I hope so', was my reply. There followed a well-rehearsed speech which I listened to patiently. My visitor was assuming that I was yet another of so many in the Highlands of that day who, misunderstanding the Gospel, did not see themselves as good enough for God and who thought it presumptuous to call oneself a Christian. That was not my problem. I was simply despairing of what I saw as my own lack of the graces I should have been displaying as a Christian. Frustrations and temptations abounded. I have read that Billy Bray, the wonderfully converted Cornish tin miner of a bygone day, once said 'The Devil knows where I live'. How I could echo his words!

God in His goodness did provide a measure of fellowship. I discovered that an elderly neighbour whom I had known from childhood, loved the Lord as I did myself and many an hour I spent at her fireside talking of the things of God. And after a couple of years, when I had got my driving licence, I met with an older church member weekly to pray for the local church which had a very small congregation and no minister. God answered our prayers! A year later a minister with his wife and five children came to occupy the manse and provided me with great friendship and fellowship.

The local District Nurse retired in 1969. She had been making daily visits to our home to help me get Mum up and dressed. The opportunity arose for me to take up that position while my salary paid for a family friend to become housekeeper for Mum and Dad. I was now the District Nurse who came each day and this lady helped me get Mum up and dressed. I even had my own home in the District Nurse's house two miles away and a car provided for work.

It was wonderful freedom! But it was short-lived. My annual leave was used to relieve the housekeeper and it was during one of those periods that, in the spring of 1970, my mother's health deteriorated rapidly and over a period of just three days she fell into unconsciousness. My sister and husband came to be with Dad and me, but it was during the night when I was taking my turn at sitting alone with her that she died. It was just weeks before her fifty-second birthday.

As the Lord had allowed it, it was a period when Billy Bray's words were particularly apt. I was not where, in my heart of hearts, I wanted to be with the Lord. I had been distracted. It was a time when I was really thankful for the teaching I had had, that I was secure in Christ, it was His holding me, not dependent on my holding on to Him. I spent many an hour on my knees, but my prayer went little further than 'Lord, keep me...'

The task of caring for Mum had been removed from me. What should I do now? My father was just four years older than Mum and, while able to look after himself, he was emotionally very dependent on me. On one occasion he had said 'You'd never get married and go and leave me, would you?'. I had come home to look after my mother. Was I now to give many more years at home for my father?

It was a Friday morning and I was reading in the book of Jeremiah chapter 17. Verses 7 and 8 spoke of the blessedness of the man whose trust is in the Lord, describing him as a tree planted by the river, whose leaves would remain green in a time of drought. I felt oppressed by a very heavy weight, sensing that drought was coming but fearing that my leaves would not remain green…

It was before the days of mobile phones. As District Nurse I had to remain at home each day until after morning surgery so that the doctor could add any new calls to my list. Being Friday and the day that I had a regular weekly call to a near neighbour of my father's, I always dropped home the weekly shopping for the housekeeper before making that call. Sadly the man did not get his bed bath that day. I found Dad to have taken a major heart attack and the doctor already called. He was too ill to be removed to hospital and a few hours later he died. "I'm not ready" was my tearful cry to the family doctor when he arrived too late in answer to my call. It was exactly four weeks from the day of my mother's funeral.

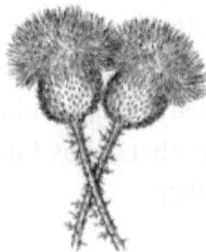

Chapter 5

Norway

'Now what?' was the inevitable question in my mind, as I so suddenly found myself relieved of family responsibilities.

Those six years earlier when I was coming to the end of formal training and considering the future, I would have loved to have joined certain friends as they made plans for Bible College with a view to service overseas. I asked myself if that was indeed God's will for me or was it simply something I would rather have done than take up my responsibility at home. I realised then that the time to discern God's will for the rest of my life would be when I was free of responsibility. And now that time had come.

In the absence of clear direction, and the need for time and space both to grieve and process all that had happened, I applied for an eight weeks' Torchbearers Bible Study course at Capernwray College in the north of England. To my surprise I learned that due to demand they were offering each course simultaneously at one of their European satellite sites. On this occasion the one I had applied for was also going to run on the island of Flekkerøy off the southern tip of Norway! That was exciting, particularly as I had always wanted to see the midnight sun. The course was to run from April to June – perfect. However, to my chagrin, I found that on checking Flekkerøy out on the map it was on exactly the same line of latitude as Helmsdale, my home village!

In spite of not experiencing sunset any later than I would have done at home, it turned out to be the most amazing experience. The off-season hotel commissioned for the course was at the water's edge. I was fascinated to find that there is no more than a six inch rise and fall of the tide in that part of the world, and the colourful houses, scattered around the island's fringe, each had their fishing boat moored at the foot of the garden. And the island boasted only two motor cars at that time, so it was blissfully serene. We were blessed with beautiful weather, no more than a handful of wet days in the two months' stay.

Many of the participants in the course were young Americans using this as 'finishing school', thus a number of years younger than me. But there were a few students nearer my own age, each there with their own reason for needing 'time out' to discern God's will for their lives. A Swedish girl was feeling pressured to become a missionary to meet her mother's own unfulfilled dream; a Dutch girl had done short-term service in Colombia and fallen in love with a young man there. Marrying him would mean living with his extended family in a remote village in that country. Should she commit? I made a particular friend of a girl from the USA, a trained nurse like me, whose grandmother had left Norway as a young girl of sixteen and never been back. She had made the treacherous sea crossing to America with others who had set up a colony where Norwegian remained the predominant language. Now a very old lady, she could still speak only broken English, but she eagerly anticipated news of the 'old country' from her granddaughter on her return. She particularly wanted to know if the cuckoo had been heard!

It was a very special time. The young Americans found the cries of the seagulls at the 3 am sunrise very disturbing! But a few of us revelled in the beauty and solitude as we had our early morning 'quiet time' sitting on the flat rocks at the water's edge.

It was not so from the beginning for me, though. Earlier I have spoken of Satan's attempt to 'sift me as wheat'. Here I am using Jesus' words to Peter in Luke chapter 22:31, words which had real meaning for me when I had read them some months earlier. Still a very new Christian, this was my first experience of the Devil's wiles, but it would certainly not be my last. He learned early on in my Christian life how to strike at my Achilles' heel, and when to do it. In this instance it was at the very time in my life when I was about to enter a period of turbulence and particularly needed God's stabilising closeness and strength. Before leaving home I had put things right that were wrong in my life and, on the basis of His Word in I John 1:9, I trusted God to have forgiven me. But forgiving myself was not so easy, and I was not experiencing peace in my relationship with God in my heart. I learned that without peace with God in one's heart beauty and serenity may not be a blessing but something of a torture.

After the evening meal one evening I chose to absent myself
from the Group activity and determined to settle the matter with
God once and for all. While all the others were actively
employed downstairs I remained in my room, on my knees
beside my bed. I laid everything out before Jesus my Saviour,
thanking Him for making it possible to know forgiveness
through what He had done for me at Calvary and asking Him to
return His peace to my heart. I don't know how long I was
there. It was the month of May in the far north so the sun set
very late. I remember it was getting dark when God answered
my agonised prayers. I had no specific verse of Scripture in my
mind when precious words were spoken to me, words which
were clearly audible to me, but I don't suppose anyone else
would have heard them if they had been in the room at that
moment. The words were the words of Jesus to the woman with
the flow of blood, when she touched the hem of Jesus' garment:
'Daughter, go in peace, your faith has made you whole'. Tears
of gratitude and joy accompanied the peace which flooded my
heart, peace which was not to be disturbed again on that
particular issue. My days of revelling in the beauty and serenity
of my surroundings on that idyllic island had begun. My journal
records on the following days that physically I was feeling well,
better than I had done for a very long time.

As we gathered at the water's edge in the early morning, each on
her own rock and with her own thoughts, prayer for God's
guidance was the priority for me. I believed that if indeed God
wanted me to serve Him overseas then I should get more

midwifery experience. It was not possible to do anything about applying from there – no internet or smartphones in those days! So, in the interest of having something to come back to while I looked into getting a job in a maternity hospital, I wrote to an address which I had in my address book. It was that of the Multiple Sclerosis Society, my mum having been a member. I asked if they had any Holiday Homes that could use voluntary help. They had – in Kent and in a convent! I enquired as to whether the establishment was Anglican or Roman Catholic. It was Roman Catholic. I prayed and was convinced I should proceed, so it was to Mary's Mead in Sevenoaks that I would go on my return from Norway.

I still had weeks of new experiences to enjoy in Norway before that day would come, however. We were invited to the annual Rekefest, the traditional shrimp feast held in the local Lutheran church. Two hundred people lined long tables laden with food. There must have been other foods on offer as shrimps would definitely not figure on my list of favourites! I remember only that it was a very enjoyable occasion.

The 17th of May was Norway's Independence Day. The roar of motor cycle engines and hooters began at 3 am. There was no sleep after that! We went into town to watch the many parades and processions, admire the women in their national costumes and listen to the many bands and choirs. Sadly it was one of the few days of rain that we had while in Norway. Following that we were taken by coach to a holiday campsite on a forested mountainside. Accommodation was in log cabins. A mountain stream ran right underneath the one I shared with three other girls. The rain continued, by this time torrential! But the cabin had a wood burning stove, so we were very cosy. Next morning we cooked our own breakfast of bacon and eggs and my journal records our pleasure at having hot tea!

Later that evening the rain cleared. Next morning I woke at 4 am and went out, keen to see the sunrise. Sadly fog from the valley below had beaten me to it. I walked close by the side of a rocky stream rushing down the mountainside. It probably wasn't very sensible. As I walked I could hear clearly in my head 'Get back! Elma, get back!' The voice was that of my father, so recently deceased, and Elma my family name.

As the sun rose the fog cleared and it revealed waterfalls and streams everywhere rushing down the mountainsides all around. It was Sunday, and we gathered as a group to worship God. In the afternoon a friend and I sat on a flat rock in the hot sunshine in such glorious surroundings and studied together Hebrews chapter 1. Verses 10-12 spoke powerfully: 'You, Lord, didst found the earth in the beginning, and the heavens are the work of your hands; they will perish but you remain; they will all grow old like a garment, like a mantle you will roll them up and they will be changed. But you are the same, and your years will never end.' We returned to our base on Flekkerøy later that evening full of thankfulness for such a wonderful experience.

All too soon our time there came to an end. The American friend I had made was going to visit friends in Sweden via

Telemark, the county of her grandmother's birth. I decided to accompany her. Together we went on to Oslo. On our final day we visited a folk museum. Of particular interest was the 'Stavekirke', the ancient church rebuilt there in its original form - the wooden building blocks interlocked so cleverly, no nails used. The wooden doorstep was deeply indented, worn away by the feet of the many who had worshipped there all those years ago. Such food for thought.

Cousins of another girl who had been with us on the course met us there and treated us to a hearty Norwegian lunch. Sadly I don't remember what exactly we had to eat, only how much I enjoyed it! We dined al fresco, our Norwegian friends under the shade of some trees while I basked in the hot sun.

Accompanied by my new friends I went straight to the railway station. There, for my American friend and I, it was the parting of the ways. I had booked for travel through the mountains on the Oslo to Bergen express, there to catch a ferry for England.

I boarded the train clad only in my sleeveless dress. The very comfortable train was fully air-conditioned. From Oslo we climbed steeply. On the platform of the highest station on the route, children were wearing woolly hats and gloves as they pushed their bicycles through rutted snow. I observed them from my railway carriage still wearing my cotton dress!

From that highest point on the journey we sped downhill past rushing mountain streams strongly reminiscent of a television advert for toothpaste, the frothy water a glorious aquamarine colour. We arrived in Bergen after 10 pm in evening twilight. A taxi took me to my destination.

The next day was Sunday. I located a service in English in the local cathedral but when I got there it was deserted! I walked for about an hour away from the town centre to Old Bergen. There I sat at the water's edge with my Bible and spent time in Psalm 103. 'Bless the LORD, O my soul; and all that is within me bless his holy name! Bless the LORD, O my soul and forget not all his benefits, who forgives all your iniquity and heals all your diseases, who redeems your life from the Pit, who crowns you with steadfast love and mercy ...' (verses 1-4). If ever I had occasion to echo those words from my heart it was then! For all of the fifty years since that day I have reckoned that solitary service sitting on a rock at the water's edge to be the most meaningful of all.

Next morning I boarded a ferry for Newcastle, England. On a bright and breezy day, I was able to view the coast of Norway from the deck of the ship as we sailed to Stavanger where I was able to disembark and look around the town. An uncomfortable and rather sleepless rocky night on a 'cushette' was unable to prevent my praising and thanking God for the wonderful experience that had been mine these eight weeks in Norway.

Chapter 6

Mary's Mead

It was a huge old mansion at the end of a long drive in thick woodland. I arrived in a stifling heatwave. It could not have been more different from either Helmsdale or Flekkerøy!

I was warmly welcomed by a sweet elderly nun wearing a white habit. Her opening words were: 'Do come and tell me, we all wonder why you've come!' She spoke with an intriguing accent - she was Norwegian!

The house was the residence of an Order of teaching nuns on leave from their work in Africa. There were ten while I was there. They did not need the whole house, so part of it became a Holiday Home for the Multiple Sclerosis Society accommodating ten guests. The President of the Society at that time was a prominent Roman Catholic whose wife had Multiple Sclerosis.

Two nursing nuns looked after the guests, one a buxom Irish lady the other my welcoming Norwegian friend. Just a day or two after my arrival, once they had decided that I could contribute what was required, this dear lady took time off and I didn't see her again while there. I was saddened to learn later that she was diagnosed with cancer and died within a few months. A young Irish girl, working during her school holidays, made up the nursing team. The teaching nuns helped with the household chores. All of them lovely people they worked extremely hard, particularly the nun who cooked for everyone.

I arrived on a Thursday. My journal for the next day reads: *'Started work at 7:30 am Really enjoyed working with the ten guests and doing general housework, all of which comes fairly natural to me.'* And for the following day, Saturday, I wrote: *'Very hot again and very busy as all guests change over completely. Sister Agnellus went to a lot of trouble to find out (from the priest!) where I could worship tomorrow. It's so easy to talk about the Lord to the sisters but I long to talk about our essential differences. Very hot, tired feet but otherwise feel very well and find the work very satisfying. Can also see what a good work the MS Society is doing, also so many ladies who give voluntary help.'*

The church suggested to me was a Baptist church in Sevenoaks. I found my way to it successfully at the end of a forty-five minute walk. It was very hot and my feet very sore. I was so glad to be given a lift home! I would happily have worshipped quietly at home in the evening, but Sister had been so impressed that anyone should want to go twice that she insisted that I get time off – and I walked both ways. That evening later was the first of many that I sat with my feet in a bucket of cold water!

During my time there I went into Sevenoaks several times, discovering that I could do so by walking through Knole Park. Knole House began as an Archbishop's Palace five hundred years ago but was taken from Thomas Cranmer by King Henry

Vlll. His daughter Queen Elizabeth 1 passed it on to her cousins the Sackville family. The hundred acre park, in which Knole House sits, is now run by the National Trust. Deer roam amongst the ancient oak trees making it a wonderful place to enjoy.

On the Monday my journal records: *'Much cooler and I am very glad. Worked 'til 4:30 and was sore! Had very good chat today with a man of 49 who has had MS since he was 18. It's such a tragic disease and is disturbing me greatly.'* This was a new experience for me. My mother had suffered from the same disease throughout my childhood but I had simply taken it as a normal part of life. I could scarcely remember her any other way. Now as an adult hearing tragic stories of loss of independence resulting in family struggles, I saw it all in a new light.

My journal continues: *'It is so much easier to talk spiritual things to the sufferers, in such a 'religious' atmosphere. Only one guest this week is Roman Catholic. I enjoy the work so much and find lots of opportunities to talk to the guests about spiritual things. They seem glad to talk. What an opportunity a Christian guest house would present!'*

I was housed in a separate building a short distance away from the main house. The only other occupant was the young Irish girl whose name I can't remember. Our rooms were such that our windows were at the level of the roadway outside. After we had settled one night, I heard footsteps on the road just outside my window. How I needed God's help to stay calm! The weather was very hot so my window was open. I was very conscious of my responsibility for the young girl in the room next door and I did not want her alarmed. I closed my window and the curtains before putting my light on. I then went and double checked that the door to the outside was locked. Now with door and window closed and my light left on, I asked God that I might sleep in spite of the circumstances – I knew how much I needed the rest for the long busy day ahead! Quite wonderfully He answered that prayer. I slept soundly until morning. My young neighbour had slept peacefully through it all. And I learned later that those on duty in the night had seen a man in the driveway…

I took my turn at being 'on call' at night, sleeping on a camp bed in the duty room. It probably wasn't very comfortable but I was so tired I slept anyway – except on the nights when I was disturbed by the call-bell ringing.

Each morning while I ate breakfast in the dining-room I could hear morning devotions being recited in the chapel on the other side of the door at my side. Lovely as those nuns were, nothing attracted me to their faith during the three weeks I was there. They were easy to talk to about spiritual things and we had many a good conversation over the washing up. One day I prayed specifically that I would have the opportunity to discuss the differences in our respective faiths. My journal records God's answer to that prayer: *'Over washing up I got into an hour-and-a-half- long discussion on the mass, salvation by*

*grace alone etc. I pray that God will give them enquiring
minds…"*

I had just got myself a copy of the newly published Amplified
Bible. The nun who worked so hard in the kitchen asked to
borrow it and one afternoon when I was off duty we had a very
profitable chat about it while sitting in the garden. A few days
later the Irish nursing nun and I were making butter balls
together in the kitchen. She confided that she was reading my
Bible and it had given her food for thought. How I was praying!

I had never lost sight of the fact that God might want
me to work for Him overseas. While waiting for His
clear leading I believed I should use the time to
prepare for such an eventuality, so after coming home from
Norway, I had applied for a post as midwife in the Kent and
Canterbury Hospital, in Canterbury and my application had been
accepted in principle. A date for interview would follow.

I had some links with Canterbury. Firstly, a young woman
slightly older than I had been working in the Aberdeen branch
of Christian Literature Crusade (CLC). She had worshipped in
'my' church and had been something of a 'Mother in Israel' to
me as Deborah was described in the book of Judges. Jose had
been relocated to the CLC shop in Canterbury in the intervening
years and had spoken of being rather lonely there. Perhaps I
could be a help to her? Then in the previous year, following my
parents' death, I had joined the Holiday Houseparty of a
missionary organisation in England's popular Lake District.

The young pastor invited to bring Bible ministry during that week chose to speak on the book of the prophet Jonah. I do not know how his ministry spoke to anyone else in our company, but I felt it was given him to preach straight from God for me. It was such a blessing! That preacher, whose wife and small children were with him, pastored a small church, also in Canterbury. And God's providence had already brought me to Kent.

Now here in Mary's Mead a letter arrived giving me a date for interview the following week. It also included an invitation to spend the night following the interview at the home of my holiday preacher! It transpired that the Superintendent Midwife was a Christian and a member of his church and that another of the midwives was a lodger in the home of Jose, my CLC friend. She also worshipped at the same church! I had made the application knowing none of this, surely God was in it all and had opened up the way? I was greatly encouraged that I was moving in accordance with His will for me.

I walked into Sevenoaks and caught the train to Canterbury on the day of my interview. I was offered the post. It was very good to renew fellowship with John and Joy White and I felt reassured that I would have good ministry to look forward to when I went to live there. I was able to visit Jose at work in the bookshop before catching the train back to Sevenoaks and a disturbed night on call.

When my time came to leave Mary's Mead, two of the nuns drove me to my new job in Canterbury. I often wondered how surprised any of my friends might have been if they'd happened to come in to the café where the three of us were having afternoon tea! I have a clear picture in my mind of the day I returned from Canterbury to visit them all. Getting off the bus and making my way down the tree-lined driveway, figures were hanging out of windows waving their enthusiastic welcome!

My time spent there was a unique experience which had God's hand clearly stamped upon it, as will be plain to see as my story unfolds…

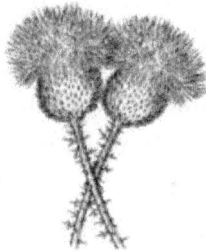

Chapter 7

Canterbury

The hospital provided accommodation in a large house on the busy Dover Road, about ten minutes' walk from the hospital, a similar distance from the church and just a bit further to walk into the city centre. Most of my fellow-residents were pupil midwives, as they were then known. I am in touch with one of them still. I had to do a spell of night duty fairly regularly. We gathered on those evenings in the little lounge where off-duty girls were relaxing with the television. A minibus taxi ferried us to the hospital. Our transport always arrived just as the signature tune of 'Coronation Street' was playing. It's not a programme I watch, but to this day if I hear that tune on television, I have a mental image of all these white-capped, navy-cloaked figures sombrely making their way out in silence! We made our own way home in the morning.

I was placed on the Labour Ward from the start. We were a teaching hospital, so not only was I expected to have full confidence in what I was doing myself, but I had to supervise the students working with me. Given that I had had no hands-on experience beyond my training several years before, it was a huge challenge. 'Their life in your hands' sort of nursing was never my favourite, I much preferred basic nursing care which can bring so much job satisfaction.

I caused quite a sensation one day. I had been left on the labour ward at lunchtime with a pupil midwife. We had one patient in labour. On doing a routine examination, I thought I felt the umbilical cord. I sent for the young house doctor who was sceptical. He used the ultrasound machine to monitor the baby's heartbeat – a fairly new innovation at the time. During a contraction, the listened-for 'thud-thud' slowed almost to a stop. The doctor tore off his rubber gloves and disappeared fast, shouting over his shoulder, 'get her ready for theatre!' I had to summon staff back from the dining room to cover the ward and sister's comment as she raced in, was something 'tongue-in-cheek' about 'so much for a midwife without experience!'. How I thanked God for enabling me! The outcome of not making that diagnosis was unthinkable. The happy mother went home with a fine healthy baby following her Caesarean Section.

I was shocked when shortly after this incident, the Superintendent announced that she wanted me upgraded to a Sister's post. I remonstrated. I really did not feel qualified and said so. But she needed another Sister on the unit and she insisted I had 'life experience'. And so a Sister I had to be. She was very put out when, on the day I should have started under the new designation, my navy uniforms hadn't been delivered. I was in no hurry to receive them!

After years of looking after home and family, 'living in' and depending on the predictable three-weekly cycle of mediocre hospital food, aggravated my sense of loss at that time. I greatly appreciated the occasional invitation to lunch at the home of the

Pastor and his young family, and even being allowed to help by doing some gardening for them now and then. During that time I bought myself a bicycle and found that in the company of colleagues, cycling up to fourteen miles in the evening after a hard day's work was perfect relaxation! I also took myself out alone on days off. The flat cornfields and apple orchards were ideal for easy cycling. Later, on a holiday back home to Scotland, on a borrowed bike, I found I could cycle back and forth to Helmsdale from Portgower without dismounting. Any reader who knows that terrain will realise it was no mean feat – but my spurt of fitness was not long-lasting!

To my surprise, my friend Jose got engaged shortly after I arrived in Canterbury. I attended the wedding with Valerie, her lodger and my fellow midwife. Valerie and I became good friends for several years. Taking a sabbatical from work in Canterbury in later years, she went to East Africa to help in a Mission hospital there. She was due home before Easter but offered to stay to relieve staff members over the holiday period. A trip was arranged to a game park. The vehicle they were in stopped to allow passengers to alight. The herd of elephants they were photographing stampeded and Valerie collapsed in their path. She was killed instantly. For her elderly parents expecting their only daughter home any day after a lengthy absence, her death was a cruel blow. The now retired Superintendent Midwife and I went to the funeral together. It was a triumphant celebration of the life of one who had loved and lived for Jesus Christ her Saviour, and who was now even more alive in Him.

Communication with family in Scotland was only by letter or the use of the communal telephone in the hall. It was on that phone that I heard the following story. I had given my pet cat to friends several miles from home nearly a year before. I had been told it wasn't settled and kept wandering off up into the hills behind the village. It would be seen and easily recognised being pure white. My friends would go and bring it back, only to have to do it again sometime later. Now I heard that it had turned up on the kitchen window sill of our family home – where with his twin brother they always waited to be let in each morning. The friendly new occupants let the cat in. He wandered all through the house, finding nothing or no-one familiar, of course. His new family was alerted and came to collect him. He didn't ever wander again. It may not surprise you that I can scarcely tell that story now sixty years later without a threatening tear… There were many at the time!

I saw my time in the midwifery department as a means of getting experience while waiting for God to show me His future plans. I had no preconception of what the future might look like, nor had I consciously formed a personal 'dream' – but one day it was revealed that unconsciously I had.

It was an unusually quiet day on the Labour Ward, no patients at all. I occupied myself by leafing through some Nursing Journals which at that time always seemed to have pages of Nursing

Homes advertised for sale. 'I wish someone would buy me one and let me run it as a Christian Home for disabled people!' was the thought which sprang unbidden into my mind. The guests at Mary's Mead had often plied the nuns with questions such as: 'Why has God allowed this to happen to me?' The answers they gave often left me dissatisfied. My time there had caused me to think deeply about such things, and of course I did not presume to imagine that I had answers in myself– I just knew that I would answer differently from my understanding of God's Word. I had suddenly recognised a desire to give loving care to such people, as the nuns certainly did, while having the opportunity to speak of God's love and offer of salvation and eternal life through Christ's death on the Cross at Calvary.

The secretary of the Exeter branch of the MS society had brought a group of people from Devon to holiday at Mary's Mead, while I was there. She stayed overnight before driving home again, and we spent several hours in conversation about MS in general (this lady's husband suffered from it, too) and the need for holidays, respite for their carers and many other things around the subject. Imagine my surprise when just two or three days after my 'lightbulb moment' on the deserted Labour Ward, I had a letter from this lady telling me that the Exeter Branch had bought a house for use as a Holiday Home for MS sufferers and they would in due course be looking for a nurse to run it. She 'knew' that I wouldn't be interested as I was in what she termed 'the mainstream of nursing', but she was asking if, in the meantime, I would come for a weekend (all expenses paid), to help their committee to think through what would be required.

In due course I went as requested to Exmouth, for that was where the Home was to be. I immediately felt at ease amongst the folk there and at home in the delightful seaside town. On leaving I asked them if they would let me know when advertising the post of Manager. I had complete peace in the conviction that this was God's will for me and was not surprised when I was chosen out of several applicants to be manager of this new work. Still a couple of months short of my thirtieth birthday, I was certainly the youngest. One of the points put at interview was that there would be no resident doctor to call on as there is in hospital. I was able to tell the interviewing panel that when I was District Nurse in the little village 'back home', I used to have to take the doctor's calls on his days off and decide whether the situation needed the doctor from the next village to be called, or not! I think that may have been a deciding factor in their minds.

When I left after a year in the midwifery department one of the midwives said: 'I can see you working day and night in that place'. Her words proved to be very close to the truth!

My final shift on the Maternity Unit was night duty. It was chaotically busy night which I replayed in my mind for days afterwards. My journal reminds me now: *'had terrible night for last night on. Had four deliveries, two normal, one breech, one Caesarean Section plus four new admissions. Didn't get off*

47

duty until 9:30 am. Got book token and signed card from the staff. Am sorry to be leaving in one way, but glad to be leaving this work. Am longing for my holiday.' I had proved again 'their life in your hands' sort of nursing was not for me. And I was excited about the different path stretching out before me.

That evening I caught the overnight train from Euston to Inverness. For the first time ever I flew from Inverness to Wick, a half-hour flight, instead of four and a half hours on the train. I was met by my sister and the five children which included the new baby I was meeting for the first time. In the afternoon, we were all on the glorious beach in the shadow of Dunnet Head, the most northerly point on the Scottish mainland, I must surely have slept well that night.

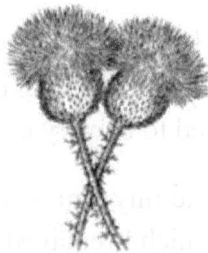

Chapter 8

Orcombeleigh

The Exeter branch of the MS Society called the house they had bought for use as a Holiday Home Orcombeleigh. It received its first full complement of eight guests on September 6th, 1972, just two days before my 30th birthday. That was probably one of the several birthdays I have experienced in life when I actually forgot my birthday! I had already spent several weeks there helping prepare for the first guests. Living alone in my little flat at the back of that big empty house was quite daunting. Tradesmen were still putting finishing touches here and there. Furniture, bedding, curtains etc were being delivered and food had to be ordered, prospective staff interviewed and appointed. It was a busy but exciting time.

The home was officially opened a few months later by Richard Cave – later Sir Richard, founder of the national MS Society and Chairman at that time. In the weeks following, I received from him a letter headed 'The House of Lords'. In the letter he was thanking me for the gift which I had been asked to present to him, but also for allowing him the use of my bedroom to 'spruce himself up', as he put it. In the letter he confessed to having had a look at my Amplified Bible and that he meant to get himself one!

Having cared for my mother at home, it was my wish – shared by the Committee – that the Home should be 'homely'. No uniforms and the least possible likeness to an institutional environment. Many guests did come from their own homes, but others came from places of care and even some from long-stay hospitals. Many were the interesting people we had the privilege of looking after for a week or two, and many were the challenges. Friendships were made that lasted long after the holiday was over and for many it became a much anticipated annual event.

Kathy was an example of both friendship and challenge. She suffered from Muscular Dystrophy. Guests with disabilities similar to MS were accepted off-season. Kathy had lived in a London hospital for years. She travelled to us in her iron lung, escorted by a nurse. It was no ordinary ambulance that brought her. The bespoke vehicle was a huge pantechnicon. With blue lights flashing and with police escort, it would speed through small towns and villages on the way from London to the West Country because her lung was dependent on the vehicle's battery for the duration of the journey. Motorway or even dual carriageway had yet to be built on that route at that time.

In spite of the hospital engineer having visited in advance to assess the suitability of our premises, it was still found to be necessary on arrival to take doors off to allow access for the iron lung! When eventually it was pushed into the spacious room with its view out over the Exe estuary, the engineer exclaimed loudly: 'You're all right, Kathy, there's a Bible here!' He had spied the Gideon's Bible on the bedside table. 'It's all right, Jim, I've brought my own', wheezed Kathy, a word or two at a time, to the rhythm of the lung's machine. Jim loved to 'rib' Kathy, having no sympathy himself for her Christian faith, but for me it was a wonderful immediate introduction to the knowledge that Kathy was a Christian.

The nurse who accompanied Kathy was familiar with her care and we worked together throughout her stay. Kathy could manage on a battery respirator for an hour or two just some days, allowing her to have an outing in a specially designed wheelchair. Orcombeleigh was close to Exmouth's lovely sea front and enjoyed glorious views of the Exe estuary. What a wonderful change from the busy North London setting of the hospital! God was gracious on that first visit, giving wonderful weather although it was still early Spring. Kathy had been ill and had plead for this holiday. Those in charge of her care had been reluctant to authorise her going so far from the hospital. She went 'home' looking so well that the medics said they'd never try to stop her going again, and she came more than once during my time there. A lovely Christian, Kathy and I became firm friends and after I moved away from Devon I took her on several holidays and cared for her in different settings. That meant that I travelled with her in that 'ambulance' and I took care to remain firmly seated beside her and not stand up to look out of the window as we travelled at speed through busy streets of shoppers on a Saturday afternoon! From time to time I also visited her in her hospital room in London while I worked in Kent. When she died some years later, she had lived twenty-five years in an iron lung…

At Orcombeleigh we invited family members to come with their loved one if they wished to – a rare treat for those who were forced to live apart in a place of care. During the week of Kathy's first visit we had a little girl come from a big city with her parents. Her mum was wheelchair bound. Kathy's nurse used time off to take the little girl to the beach. The first time they went the tide was out and there was lots of sand. The next time they went the tide was in. Unfamiliar with the beach, the sea and the tides, she asked 'When is the beach open?'

A lovely young policeman was a regular visitor. On one occasion his wife, a policewoman, came with him. She was a gentle, quiet person who spent most of the time beside John in his room. I did not get to know her well then, but such was her appreciation of the care her dearly loved husband had received, that years later, when she wrote to tell me sadly of John's death, she asked 'Please may I be a friend for my own sake?' We kept in touch and, years later, she visited me in Northern Ireland. Her lovely son, the image of his father, wrote to tell me of his mother's death from cancer not so long ago.

How interesting were the conversations with the lovely Jewish lady who had lost so many professional and talented family members in the Holocaust, and what happy memories of Arthur, a big man in every way although blind and helpless, always wielding a padded stick in the hand that had some movement, so he could scratch his nose! Arthur had a great sense of humour and a fund of jokes that kept everyone smiling. Phyllis, too, was blind as well as helpless due to MS. She blamed her blindness on the crying she did when her fiancé was killed in the war.

These were incredibly busy but very happy years. However, an extension to the Home resulting in the need for more staff and more administration took me further from those in my care. Furthermore, there were calls for me to organise evenings out to the pub for the guests and an annual fund-raising garden party to be held on Sundays. That, combined with the lack of young Christians for fellowship in the dormitory town of Exmouth and my failure to find a place of worship that wholly satisfied my hunger for spiritual food, led to my becoming restless and again looking to God for direction.

My ideal would have been a similar work in a wholly Christian setting, but as far as I was aware there was no such place to be found anywhere in the UK at that point in time. God made sure I didn't miss it when one such holiday home was established in years to come – but more of that in a later chapter!

In the meantime, as I waited and prayed, the 'Urgently required' advertisement placed by the Aged Pilgrims' Friend Society (now Pilgrims' Friend Society), seemed to come up before me in each and every Christian publication I read. In the end I succumbed, and it was to care for the elderly that I went back to Kent, this time to Tunbridge Wells in West Kent, on the border with East Sussex. I was to manage one of the two Homes run by the APFS in that town.

It was November 1975 when I set off in my Renault 4 (the so-called 'Mountain goat'), to drive from west to east, from Devon to Kent. I had begun to acquire 'stuff' by this stage, not just a vehicle! The car was well packed up, including the cage containing my black cat Peter, suitably tranquilised for the long journey…

Chapter 9

The Nursing Home

'If I have plumbed new depths during these years, so I have reached new heights of proving God's faithfulness and love'. These were words I used when I came to move on more than five years later – but here I am, just arrived, and these heights and depths have yet to be experienced!

I had come from an establishment newly appointed; I had come to one well-worn, and tired. I had come from one with an attractive big front garden and glorious views toward the sea; I was now in a built-up area with little outlook and no garden to speak of. I had come from a team that I had had a part in bringing together; my new team were 'old hands' who were understandably uncertain if not a little suspicious of this latest in a long line of 'new Matrons'. It was not an immediate 'marriage made in heaven'. God had His moments of encouragement for me, though, and I loved Him for them. One such was a cold snowy day outside. Inside I was in my very small and rather dark 'Matron's office'. The window looked out into a big tree in the neighbour's garden. There on the bark of the tree, contrasting with the snow, was a red and black spotted woodpecker. My heart said, 'Thank you, Lord!'

I arrived late November, Christmas just around the corner. I didn't know the town or the shops, so I was grateful for someone's offer to shop for what was needed for Christmas dinner (catering and housekeeping was part of my remit, as also was doing the cooking when the cook didn't turn up). And so began a succession of Christmases, allowing the mainly married staff as much time off as possible while I gave myself to my new family of Nursing Home residents, all twenty-one of them or as many as could not spend it at home with family members. I made it my practice to have everything ready by early on Christmas Eve, then to take myself off to the great outdoors for the day. Seaforde Head on the East Sussex coast was a favourite spot. I could climb the steep path up and along the white chalk cliffs or keep to the valley bottom where the river meandered to the sea. It was there I saw my first ever wheatear with its distinctive black and white tail. Perhaps not at Christmas, though!

I had kept in touch with a friend who shared a house with several others near Canterbury. Peter the cat and I often went there for days off. Remarkable cat that he was, he leapt out of his basket from the boot of the car on arrival and spent his time doing who knows what or where until the time came to go home, when he always appeared on cue and joined me in the car again for the 90-minute journey home! He couldn't come with me, though, when later my friend rented a flat in the Archbishop's palace beside the Cathedral in Canterbury city centre. On one notable occasion, when I drove at crawling speed through the crowded pedestrian precincts on a Sunday afternoon, the current Archbishop himself, out for a walk with his wife, opened the Palace gates for me, saving me the trouble!

It was on one of those visits that one day my friend and I went in search of blackberries in a nearby wood. She had lent me a pair of her jeans for the task. Being taller than I was, I bent over to roll them up at my ankles – and couldn't straighten up. I was not in pain at that stage, but there was nothing for it but to get back into her car and go home.

It was as she drove us back towards Canterbury that the pain set in – and how! It was impossible to straighten up or to walk at all without help. As soon as the news reached my colleagues and friends I was inundated with messages leaving me various telephone numbers of recommended osteopaths or chiropractors. A couple of excruciating visits to one or other only made matters worse. So there followed a period of several months of being cared for by the staff of the Home while I spent many weeks in bed. My thirty-fifth birthday was marked during that time – though there was little celebration. The time of rest and 'living within my limits' did improve matters, although there was no 'cure' as back pain became a feature of life from that time on.

I had plenty of time to consider why this might have happened. A contributing factor would have been the years of caring for my mother at home during her final years of Multiple Sclerosis, before the availability of hoists (at least, not in the Highlands of Scotland!), and long before the 'No Lifting Policy' had been thought of. The years of hard physical work and long hours in Orcombeleigh would also have played a part. I remembered, too, that on the days before the blackberry expedition, we had been short-staffed in the Nursing Home. Having worked all of one day, the night nurse did not turn up and a substitute could not be found, so I simply worked on until the next morning. My deputy was either off sick or on holiday and I had to remain 'on call' even when off duty the next day, and I had used some of the time when I couldn't leave the building to work in the shrubbery at the front of the house. It was time to trim the shrubs. I remember I would bend over to use the shears on the lower ones, then have to walk in the stooped position to straighten up against one of the pillars on the veranda to ease my back, then go back and carry on with the task. Yes, lessons have been learned since then!

Added to all of that I do believe there was another dimension to the problem of stress and tension in my body. The elderly patients in the Nursing Home were all professing Christians, but sadly, old age does not find all of us sweet and easy to deal with – would that it were so! Of course Satan was going to be active in a work that set out to honour God, and God knew that I needed to be refined and sanctified, too. Sometimes there were personality clashes within the staff team, as well. I used to say that caring for the dear elderly folk (and I did get very fond of them all), was easy, I had been trained for that, but supporting members of staff in their personal lives as well as their work was certainly a challenge. Not for the first time in life I had cause to remember the words attributed to Billy Bray, the wonderfully converted Cornish miner, 'The devil knows where I live' – he knew where I lived, too! I was spiritually dry.

The senior person on duty was responsible for leading everyone in devotions and prayer each afternoon before tea. All gathered in the little ward of eight beds for that time. On at least five days of every week that task fell to me. During that period when I had allowed things into my life which had edged God to the periphery, it was such a good discipline to have to focus on God's Word and to pray.

During that 'desert' experience God presented me with a challenge – I was asked by a local Church ladies' group to speak to them about how I had come to put my trust in Jesus and to tell something of what He had done in my life. 'I can't do that, not right now!' I cried. Yet I knew that I could not possibly refuse. I had to come humbly before God and ask His mercy and His grace, and He did not refuse me. What a gracious God we have! This turned out to be one of the 'heights' I spoke of at the beginning of this chapter, for God brought a peace beyond understanding into my heart and gave me a totally up-to-date testimony to the reality of our God to present to these ladies from a full and thankful heart.

God knew, though, that I had things to put right in my life and that the peace He had given me was for the specific purpose of bringing glory to Him in the giving of that talk. Afterwards the turmoil returned until He brought me to the place of being willing to be obedient to Him. That meant making agonising decisions and taking action that felt completely beyond my ability to carry out. Determined as I was to be obedient, my faithful God once again stepped in and brought a supernatural calmness and strength that carried me through the particularly difficult days, a time that proved to be amongst the highest of the experiences of Him that I have known.

Five years had passed and it seemed now to be time to move on, but fearing lest I further grieve the God who had shown such love to me, I determined not to take a step in any direction until I could be sure of moving in His will. As I waited I considered and I prayed. My choice would have been to return to working amongst the younger disabled, this time in a Christian context, but still I knew of no such work. Approaching forty years of age by this time, I would have been glad to have my own home – I had been living 'on the job' for ten years. I looked at any advertisement I saw for someone to manage a Christian Nursing Home and did see one in Buckinghamshire – a beautiful county, I knew, but land-locked, and the thought came unbidden: 'O, Lord, please don't take me further from the sea than I am already!' Tunbridge Wells was a ninety minute drive from the sea. I had grown up by the sea and had lived more than three years by the sea in Devon.

Having lived through a few turbulent years it seemed I was now hankering after my roots. I could only present these random thoughts to God in prayer and wait, as month followed month.

Christmas 1980, my sixth in Tunbridge Wells, rolled over into the New Year of 1981...

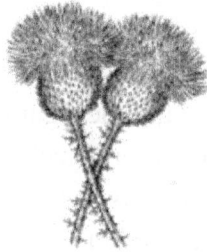

Chapter 10

A Sunday Evening Phone Call

The residents of the Nursing Home always settled early so the house was very quiet, making the evening feel later than it actually was. It was early January so very dark, and being Sunday evening, it was even quiet outside. I sat in my rocking chair thinking about nothing in particular. My reverie was disturbed by the ringing of the telephone at my elbow. 'Is that Wilma Nicolson?' I was asked in an unfamiliar accent. Being assured that the caller had got the right person, they went on to ask if I had heard from Jennifer Frizelle. Now Jennifer and I were fellow midwifery students in Edinburgh many years before. She was from Belfast but we had kept in touch because, even as a student midwife, she had already been diagnosed with Multiple Sclerosis. My mother having had the same condition, Jenny and I had a particular connection. I had had a Christmas card from Jennifer, nothing more, although she had apparently told Claire – for that was my caller's name – that she would write to me. On learning that I had not had a letter from Jenny, Claire went on to explain – 'We are a Christian family in Northern Ireland who run a Holiday Home for disabled people and we are looking for a nurse'. I voiced the question which sprang spontaneously to mind: 'What accommodation could you offer?' That desire to have a home of my own had obviously taken a greater priority than even I myself had realised. The reply caught my attention immediately: 'We would not require you to live in, you would have to find your own accommodation'. Claire then added as something of an afterthought 'Oh, by the way, the house is just fifty yards from the sea'. The three desires of my heart – a Christian Holiday Home for the disabled, close to the sea, and the opportunity to have my own home, all presented to me in a few short sentences! Surely God was in this?

Although she had never spoken of it to me, Jenny had frequently stayed at Wayside – the name given to this Holiday Home. I had written on my Christmas card to her a few weeks earlier that I was ready for a move if the Lord were to open a door. Jenny knew that I had experience of caring for people with a disability, so when she heard that Wayside's previous nurse had left she immediately telephoned to tell them about that message on my card. Andy, Claire's husband and head of the Home, had been fasting and praying about their urgent need. Jenny's call came on Saturday, the final day of his fast. The next day, Sunday, Andy's daily Scripture reading took him to Genesis chapter 24, the account of Abraham's servant being sent to another country to find a wife for his son, Isaac. Andy, sensing God's direction in this reading, resulted in my phone ringing that Sunday evening!

All of that I was to learn later, of course, but in the meantime I was much in prayer about this remarkable turn of events.

Friends with whom I shared agreed with me that there was 'too much of the Lord in it to be able to afford to ignore it' and so, after a few days, I let it be known that I was willing to consider their need as an answer to my own prayers.

The family knew that it was important that they should meet this one who might become the new member of their team – but how could they expect someone to travel from Kent to Northern Ireland in February? What they didn't know was that I already had holiday booked in February and was going to meet a friend in Scotland. Furthermore, my time off began a full weekend before my friend's leave began, and so I was free to travel to Scotland via Northern Ireland, and that is what I did.

At the end of my first ever flight, I was met by Andy at Belfast International Airport. Conversation during the forty-five minute car journey to Donaghadee flowed easily and naturally, as, in fact, it continued to do over the weekend that I spent with the family. As well as Andy and his wife Claire and their two little girls, I was introduced to Claire's sister Dorothy and their mother, widow of David Ravey, founder of the work at Wayside.

Wayside had begun life as the home of carpet magnate Cyril Lord. The fragments of his private jetty where he moored his yacht were opposite the driveway. The rooms in this large modern mansion were spacious – perfect for wheelchairs – and the views from the floor-to-ceiling picture windows magnificent. The sea shore was virtually at the foot of the lawned garden. The largest and nearest of the Copeland Islands, with its deserted cottages and sheep in the green fields, was to me strongly reminiscent of the setting of my Granny's cottage in the most northernly county of Caithness in Scotland, where I happily spent my summer holidays as a child.

I had the opportunity to walk along the broad promenade-like pavement into the small town of Donaghadee, population of just under seven thousand, a short distance to the south. There I saw its splendid lighthouse at the harbour and sampled an ice cream. I learned that further down the east coast of the Ards peninsula were a succession of small towns, each with its own harbour. Not at all unlike the east coast of Sutherland where I had grown up.

 I felt very much at home!

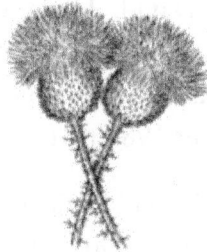

Chapter 11

David Ravey's Story

Andy, Claire and I spent much time in conversation over that weekend and I learned a lot more about the story behind Wayside. It had been the fruit of God's leading of Claire's father, David Ravey. David had experienced a lengthy period of depression during which time he questioned the sincerity of his faith in God. He was convinced he had been a hypocrite and was now under God's judgement.

Claire had already begun to write her father's story. That book is now in circulation and I can quote from it: 'As far as David could see he was lost, lost, eternally lost…This state of fear and despair persisted for two long years until gradually it came to him that all a hypocrite needed to do was to recognise hypocrisy as sin. He was a sinner. And Jesus always received sinners… All harsh condemnation was gone as Jesus gently whispered: "Your sins are forgiven, David. I gave you eternal life and you shall never perish. Nobody can snatch you out of My hand. But don't forget, my sheep listen to my voice and they follow me."' (A Faith that Goes Further 1989 p.16)

David now realised that he had made all decisions in his life to this point without reference to God. He determined that that would now change. My reader would have to read the book to hear about the path David was led along as he prayed and read the Scriptures and listened for God's voice and direction. Eventually the time came when he read the story of George Müller, the man who rescued hundreds of destitute children from the streets of Bristol and housed and fed them.

Again I quote from Claire's book: 'He (David) was fascinated. The principles by which Müller lived were rooted in the Scriptures and through the story David was reminded of the time when God had first deluged a shower of divine promises on him. Christ had been beckoning him to enter into the experience of these and how better could he prove the Word of God reliable in day to day living than by trusting God to supply his every practical need like George Müller. "Lord, I want to walk by absolute faith in You from this day forward. I will take Your Word not just as a spiritual light but as a literal light to my daily path. You know all my future and are quite capable of dove-tailing Your Word to apply it to my daily circumstances. Lead me and show Yourself to be the God who keeps His promises as He did for George Müller. I will never tell a human soul when I am in need, for you know all things. Make my life a living proof of Your power to provide every time whether for the work You will show me to do or for my own family."' (p.21). And the work God showed him to do was to minister to disabled people by providing a place for them to enjoy fellowship and holiday while hearing God's Word – and that place was Wayside.

Although I felt very much 'at home' that weekend, I realised that were I to uproot myself from the south of England and move 'lock, stock and barrel' to Northern Ireland I would not easily be able to change my mind if I found I had made a mistake!   I would have to be utterly convinced that this was God's will for me and I wanted nothing else. I would be much in prayer.

I now know that Andy was also remembering that in the story of Genesis chapter 24 the maiden that Abraham's servant would approach, if she were God's choice, would be a willing worker and willing to go with him to his master's country.   I told Andy that he would have to wait until I knew what God would have to say to me and his reply conveyed that as a family they wanted only God's choice and that they were used to waiting for God to lead and guide. They, too, would be much in prayer!

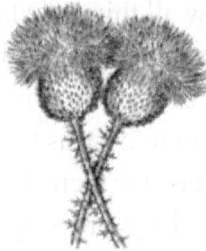

Chapter 12

Jeremiah

Monday morning found me on what would be the first of many trips across the Irish Sea on the Stena Line passenger ferry. The nearly three-hour crossing was then followed by a long train journey to the north of Scotland.

Such a journey always needs a good book and I had brought one that I had been given as a Christmas present just weeks before. Could the giver ever have known how appropriate that book would be? But God knew! It was written by WEC missionary to the Congo (as it was then known), Dr Helen Roseveare. The title was 'Living Faith', and living faith was exactly what was going to be required if indeed God was calling me to this new work. David Ravey and the team at Wayside looked to God alone to supply their need. If I were to join the team I would be paid the same wage as I was already receiving in my current position, but only as God supplied.

Here in this book I was introduced to another in Dr Helen Roseveare who looked to God alone to meet her every need. How my heart was challenged! Was God asking me to walk this same path? I was reminded of the similar challenge I experienced as a very young Christian many years before on meeting these WEC students in Aberdeen, spoken of in an earlier chapter of this book.

I was met at Carrbridge train station in Inverness-shire by my good friend and erstwhile fellow student nurse, Elizabeth. The nearby guest house was very comfortable and, being February and 'low season', we had the lounge with its cheerful log fire to ourselves. In the evenings we enjoyed each other's company while chatting and playing Scrabble. By day we took long walks and drank in the winter beauty of my native Scottish Highlands. One particular memory is of Loch Morlich with the snow-covered Cairngorm mountains beyond and ducks skating on top of the frozen water of the loch. Another is of a circular walk around Loch Dearg when we walked some distance apart, each lost in her own thoughts – mine centred on the events of recent days and what the future might hold.

I sought God's will for me in the way I had always done, by praying as I read the Scriptures day by day while all the while asking God to speak to me through His Word.

I had begun at that time to read the book of Jeremiah, a book which those years ago I was not as familiar with as I am now. The early part of the book is chapter after chapter of God's righteous judgement pronounced on the people of Israel because of their sin. Knowing my own sinful heart and how I had not been following Him as closely as I knew I should, it was hard to read. I was tempted to read elsewhere, but I have always believed that God speaks to us through our regular faithful reading of His Word and so I persisted in my reading of Jeremiah.

At that time I didn't know that in chapter 29 God's theme of condemnation turns to one of reconciliation and restoration. It was on the very last day of that holiday that I came to chapter 31 where verse after verse spoke personally in a very powerful way. After a few years of going my own way and feeling I fully deserved the voice of condemnation in earlier chapters I now heard oh, so reassuringly: 'I have loved you with an everlasting love; therefore I have continued my faithfulness to you' (v.3); 'I will turn their mourning into joy, I will comfort them and give them gladness for sorrow'(v.13); 'My people shall be satisfied with my goodness'(v.14); 'There is hope for your future, says the LORD'(v.17); 'I have heard Ephraim bemoaning, "You have chastened me and I was chastened...bring me back that I may be restored, for you are the LORD my God. After I had turned away I repented... I was ashamed and I was confounded because I bore the disgrace of my youth." Is Ephraim my dear son? Is he my darling child? For as often as I speak against him, I do remember him still. Therefore my heart yearns for him; I will surely have mercy on him, says the LORD' (vv.18-20). By this time the tears were flowing freely as I read. All the while I had been looking for something that would say to me 'this is the way, walk in it...', instead God knew what it was I needed. I needed to trust Him!

He spoke love and comfort to my bruised and battered heart and I was ready to respond when I read the crunch-line: 'How long will you waver, O faithless daughter?' as v.22 is rendered in the

Revised Standard Version which I was using. God was asking
me to trust him, and I was ready to say 'Yes, LORD, I will'.

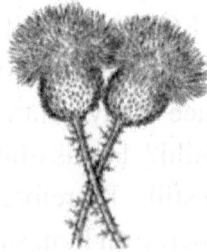

Helmsdale

Leaving home at 18

With Joan at 'Elsie's'

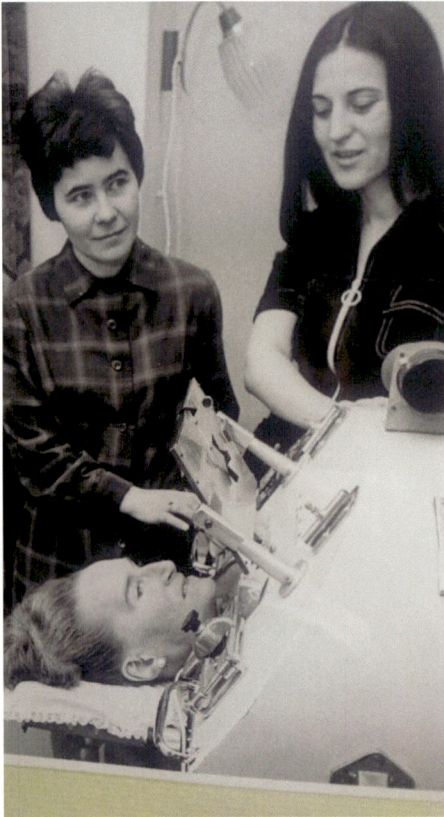

With Kathy in her iron lung

Wayside

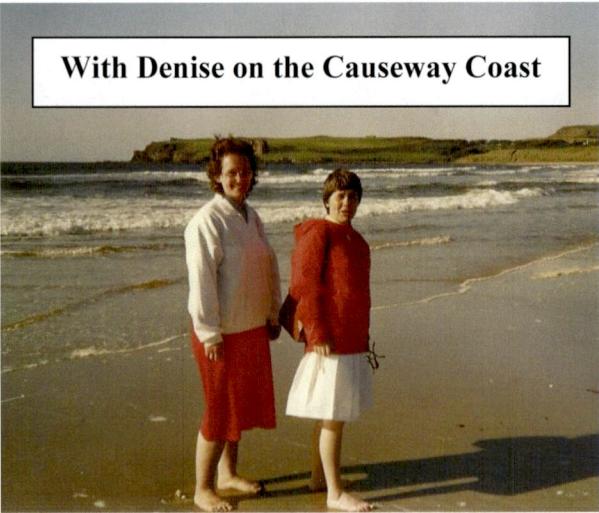

With Denise on the Causeway Coast

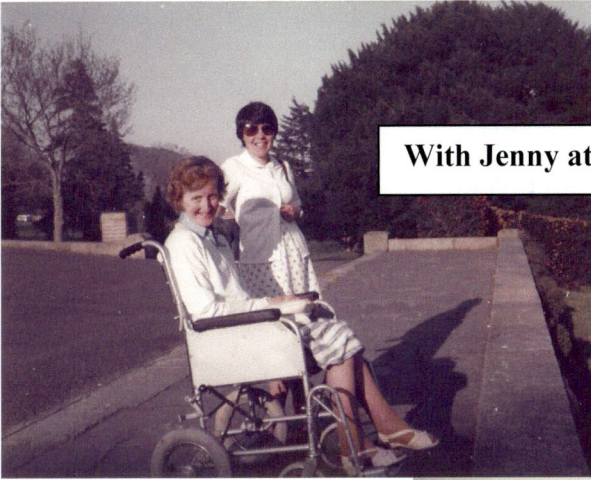
With Jenny at Tollymore Forest Park

At home with Marlene and Dusty

Elizabeth Mantell at No. 75

The Mountain Goat at No. 75

Sarah and Cherrie in my back garden

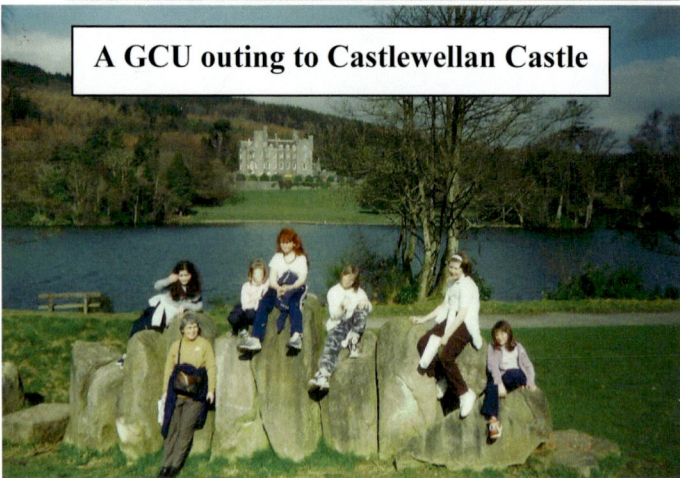

A GCU outing to Castlewellan Castle

Chapter 13

Relocation

Returning to Tunbridge Wells with decision made, my resignation had to be written. It was going to be very hard for me to do and I hesitated, asking God for needed help. How was I going to be able to leave the folk for whom I had had responsibility for years and whom I had come to love? Adding to my difficulty was the fact that the recently appointed assistant Matron hadn't settled and had already left!

It was the evening of March 7th, 1981. At that time I was using the little book of daily Scripture readings entitled 'Daily Light on the Daily Path'. I picked it up to read the evening selection. 'My times are in your hands'– that was for me. 'All His saints are in your hand' – that was for them! God was in control of their circumstances as He was of mine. That resignation letter had to be written, and written it was.

The search for somewhere for me to live in Northern Ireland began. Once again it was late evening and once again I was sitting in my rocking chair beside the telephone when it rang. Claire was telling me about an advertisement she had seen and responded to. A business man was seeking a tenant for a 'superior' flat in a block he owned. He had just returned that evening from a business trip and was setting off again for London the next morning and wanted an answer. This particular flat he had furnished for his daughter, hence 'superior', but it was situated on the edge of a town a number of miles of twisty country roads away from Donaghadee. Access was next to an industrial site and by an outside stairway to first floor level. He also wanted a year's commitment. It didn't sound ideal. And I was not used to making such a big decision in haste – yet the friends at Wayside, while working under-staffed, were taking time out of their busy schedule to search on my behalf for somewhere for me to live. Perhaps on this occasion I was being forced to make a hasty decision and end their quest by saying 'yes' to this proposal.

I picked up the telephone to convey this news. It was dead! Hadn't I had Claire's call less than an hour before? It was long before the days of mobile phones. There was a public telephone downstairs in the hall for the use of residents and staff. I gathered up some change and went to use it. The coins dropped right through the box with a clang and out again without making any connection. Yet no fault had been reported to me, the one responsible. Back upstairs I tried my phone again – still dead. I sat in silent wonderment beside it, overwhelmed by the sense that God was in control…

After a few more unsuccessful attempts I decided it was now too late to make a call, I would just have to let this flat go. But I checked my phone one more time before retiring to bed – and there was the missing dialling tone! That tangible sense of God being present by His Spirit and of His being at work on my behalf remained with me as I went to rest and was re-affirmed next morning when I checked the coin box in the hall – nothing wrong with it at all. God had stepped in… Surely He had something better prepared for me?

Busy weeks followed, during which it was arranged that for my early weeks I could make use of a room in Wayside while I set about finding myself somewhere to make a permanent home. In the meantime, Andy and Claire had occasion to share at a meeting about my impending arrival to join their team. A man approached them afterwards to ask if he could help. He had a furniture business with a van going back and forth to London. Could his driver bring my things over? He could indeed!

On Easter Tuesday towards the end of April 1981 I set off with my little Renault 4 packed to the roof with what I needed for immediate use in Wayside. Included as an essential was my rocking chair, it's excellent support so important for my often aching back.

I left Tunbridge Wells very early in the morning in order to get through the city before rush-hour; the orbital M25 motorway was still in the minds of the planners. I stopped to visit Kathy in her iron lung in Hendon Hospital, north London, saying my 'goodbye' while feeding her breakfast. Little did I know it was to be my very last visit to Kathy, although we went on to have regular lengthy telephone chats. Some months later dear Kathy was found one morning to have slipped away to be with Jesus.

It was very shocking for those of us who knew her and loved her, but for her it was 'better by far'. It was a privilege to be able to be one of the large crowd of friends who attended her funeral – she had only five relatives. 'Out of circulation' for twenty-five years, limited in speech while permanently confined to her iron lung, she had made a huge impact on all who had any contact with her. Members of the Hendon constabulary, who had always accompanied her special ambulance whenever she left the hospital, sought 'the privilege of accompanying her on her last journey'. Two gleaming white outriders led the funeral procession followed by a limousine carrying high-ranking police officers. It was incredibly moving and tears prick my eyelids even as I write this many years later.

But I'm digressing! I pull myself back to that first-ever car journey north from Kent to Northern Ireland. Breaking my journey overnight in Dumfries I left early the next morning to drive due west to Stranraer for the ferry crossing to Larne. Something under an hour's drive after disembarking later that afternoon I arrived safely at Wayside. How thankful I was! Finding Claire hanging washing on the line, I was warmly welcomed by her and all the other members of the family.

A large bed-sit was made available to me, its huge floor-to-ceiling and wall-to-wall window flooding the room with light. With its view of the swimming pool and the daffodil-framed grassy slope rising to the trees behind, this magnificent room would become my comfortable home for my early weeks in Northern Ireland.

The dressing rooms Cyril Lord had built above the swimming pool were also in my view. One of those rooms was now Andy's designated prayer room and seeing the light on in there at regular intervals throughout each day was to prove a great comfort to me, as were the prayers of the team as we gathered each morning, one and another asking God to lead and guide to the place of His choosing to be my permanent home. It was a source of strength to me to have the support of others as I prayed about where I should live. I sensed I was not alone.

I had not always had such encouragement! 'There's no future for this Province', was the discouraging remark from one good friend who had ministered to me in Scotland but who had since returned to his native Ulster. But God's Word had something to say to me. My reading in Jeremiah had taken me on from chapter 31 to chapter 32, where God asked the prophet to buy a piece of land in the very place over which he had been pronouncing God's judgement, foretelling its abandonment as the people would be taken off into exile in Babylon. God's instructions were that he should buy the field but take the deed of purchase and bury it where it would be safe for a very long time. Through the prophet, God was telling the people that in years to come they would return and the land would again be inhabited.

This Scripture encouraged me that, in spite of the precariousness of my finances, as seen through human eyes, and the commitment it meant I would be making to my future in Northern Ireland, I should buy a house. 'A mortgage will be a millstone round your neck', was another comment designed to discourage.

Within weeks of arriving in Northern Ireland I had found 75, Silverstream Crescent in Bangor, reduced in price 'for a quick sale' the very day I saw it, to £17, 750. My offer of the asking price was immediately accepted. A three-bedroom end-of-terrace with garden front and back and off-road parking, it was just off the dual-carriageway 'ring road' around Bangor, making for a straightforward six-mile drive to work in Donaghadee each day. It would become my home for the next twenty-one years, but much more about that later!

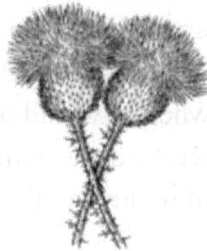

Chapter 14

Wayside

A year after I arrived at Wayside, Marlene joined us to complete the team. A short time later she joined me in 75, Silverstream Crescent. She needed somewhere to live, too, and as I had a spare room it became her lodgings. This was a considerable step of faith on my part, having lived 'on the job' in previous places of employment and knowing only too well how 'tricky' relationships could be, I went into this new arrangement deliberately and determinedly trusting God for the outworking of it. Some thirteen years later, following her Mother's death and with no need to travel to an empty house in County Antrim for off-duty days, Marlene sold the family home and bought a house not far from mine in Bangor. It's now more than forty years since we first met and we remain close friends. We have always had diverse 'down time' interests. I have never shared Marlene's love of shopping but, being a few years younger than me, I greatly appreciate her help with shopping now that I am older and without a vehicle of my own! In spite of such differences we have always been completely at one where the things of God are concerned. Marlene's friendship and support was to prove invaluable over the years, and my need of that will become clear in the chapters to follow.

Guests came to Wayside for a two-week stay, Saturday to Saturday. On the day of their departure the team would set about clearing up and leaving the house in readiness for a new group a week later. This meant a three-weekly cycle of fifteen consecutive days (ten hours minimum), on duty and six days off. The working day began at 7:45 am with a team prayer time. Marlene and I alternated between two 'shifts'. On one we had the afternoon off, returning for the evening meal at six o'clock and working until everyone was settled for the night, usually around 10:30 pm. On the alternative shift we would work right through the day until after the evening meal. We all ate as a family around the polished board-room table in the dining-room where its mirrored wall reflected the marvellous view of the Copeland Islands surrounded by the sea. Andy often regaled us all with the quip: 'When you can see Scotland it's going to rain, and when you can't see Scotland it *is* raining'. Such is the weather in Northern Ireland! These were cheerful times and no-one left the table hungry after enjoying Dorothy's wonderful home cooking, often the talking point of the guests.

A few weeks into my new role my journal entry reads: *'Had very good chat with Claire and Andy, when I told them that I had no doubts at all that the Lord meant me to be there, with which they quickly and sincerely agreed that neither had they'*. And that remained true as the weeks and months passed, in spite of the work being demanding and often challenging. One of the constant challenges was the need to trust the Lord to meet the financial need. If the need of the work was not met then I wouldn't get paid, at least, not on time. Occasionally that is just what happened. How thankful I was for God's confirming His calling to me in so many different ways so that I was enabled to trust Him! Another journal entry at such a time reads: *'Took guests for a run to Portavogie. A glorious day – daffodils in bloom, lambs in the fields, ploughing in progress, far horizons clear beyond the blue sea and my passengers, more usually housebound, enjoying it with me. It all reached to the depths of my being and my heart said: "Wages or no wages, thank you, Lord, for bringing me here."'*

While working hard on a daily basis with the team and groups of guests, I was also 'playing hard' on the weeks in between. The house needed redecorating and I tackled that as soon as I moved in, but it wasn't finished in a day. How I was appreciating and enjoying having my own home! I sometimes wondered if it was possible to weary the Lord with my thanks repeated over and over again to Him continually. I loved working in the garden and as the years went by I enjoyed harvesting potatoes, carrots, leeks, strawberries and even on at least one occasion purple sprouting broccoli – none of those particularly successful or blemish-free, but I was happy!

The bare wall of a neighbour's garage formed one boundary of my garden. Eventually it was covered over completely with pyracantha which was ablaze with bright red berries every winter and clematis 'montana' in the summer. I tried hard to grow sweet pea and did produce enough to enjoy it's delightful fragrance each year, but was never as successful as I would like to have been. It was very satisfying to plant hydrangea and mahonia shrubs and a bottlebrush tree amongst other things. I watched them mature and eventually produce their flowers year by year.

I loved to entertain, too. On my 'days off' and during the summer I often had friends from 'across the water' to visit. Life was full and satisfying. As I write this in my eightieth year – and 'feeling my age'– I marvel at a particular journal entry in 1984. It was a Saturday so Wayside must have been having a holiday break. This is how it reads: *'Cooked in the morning, also planted two rows of potatoes. Collected Harry McAllister from his home in town and had him and Joe Livingstone (my neighbour whose wife was visiting relatives in Canada) for lunch. Took Harry to visit his wife in Downpatrick Hospital, returned 5:15 and dropped him home. Had Andy, Claire and the girls for tea. At 8 o'clock went for a game of Scrabble with Margaret Young. Home 11 pm and put final coat of polyurethane on the dining-room chairs.'* Phew, what it was to be young!

I learned so very much during the four and a half years I worked at Wayside, not least about trusting God. I learned from team members as I observed their quiet trust in testing times. Over and over again I saw God's faithfulness as he continually stepped in and made provision as needs were brought to Him daily. Part of my role was to look after holiday bookings. We often got a request from a Social Worker to have one of their clients to stay. 'They don't have much money', they might say. I had to exercise my confidence in God as I would reply 'Oh, that's all right as we do not make a charge', even while knowing that at that particular juncture funds were low – sometimes very low!

I will share one story – one of many such stories – to illustrate. We were several weeks behind in our wages; the telephone bill was due to be paid and there was little money available to shop for provisions. One morning in my personal devotional time before work I had come in my Scripture reading to 2 Kings chapters 6 and 7. The city of Samaria was under siege and what food there was available was exorbitantly expensive. The prophet Elisha came to the King of Israel and told him that the very next day food would be plentiful and cheap. An army captain at the King's right hand said: 'If the Lord himself were to make windows in heaven, could this thing be?' (chapter 7 v. 2). At that point in my reading I said to myself that if God were to meet our need that day it would be as great a miracle as then. I went in to work and Andy put a wage-packet in my hand. 'But Andy', I said, 'What about the telephone bill?' Andy replied that he believed it right to use the money at hand to give us a week's wages and continue to trust God for the rest. He went on to say: 'And when I had done that another gift came which paid the telephone bill'. I worshipped God and have never again read that story in the Scriptures without thinking of that other Wayside story. He is the same real, personal, wonder-working God today as He was then!

Chapter 15

Changes!

It was Spring 1985. I was four years into the busy cycle of fifteen days on and six days off – six days which never seemed to be long enough to get fully rested and feel ready to start again. While already 'under par' a virus of some sort struck and I was forced to take time off work. It began during a week off. I returned to work as planned on the Saturday but had to come home again on the Sunday. Two courses of antibiotics did not improve matters and each attempt to return to work resulted in coming home again. Blood tests then showed several abnormalities suggesting a viral infection, and it was a relief to know there was something amiss and I could relax and rest.

Week after week followed during which I had energy only to get up and get myself something to eat. Church friends, when they learned what was happening, were wonderful. On a number of occasions one poor man, on returning home from work, was sent by his wife straight back across town with a plated hot meal for me, microwave ovens were yet to be invented!

It was a spring and summer of very indifferent weather. I remember a particularly cold spell in May when the tiny patch of sea visible between rooftops from my front bedroom window revealed snow-covered hills on the coast of Scotland beyond. The sun seldom appeared to tempt me out. Mostly I was content to lie quietly and dose but as the weeks passed I began to feel able to read and pray again and, needless to say, I was asking God what He had in store for me. As the weeks passed and I felt able to be up and about a bit and go to church, the question became more and more urgent. He had so clearly brought me to this place and given me a home which I loved. I could not contemplate moving again. Yet I could not contemplate returning to working long days either. He would have to show me clearly just as He had done four years earlier and I must be patient and listen carefully for His voice.

Wayside, meantime, was in a testing situation. Provision had not been made for wages to be paid for several weeks. As leader of the work, Andy's faith was being stretched as he felt the responsibility to pay the staff. The faith of each of us due to be paid was also being stretched. Andy often said that if God wanted to test the faith of any one of us then all had to be equally tested. We had not had wages for several weeks, but my needs had been met in a variety of ways. This prompted me to consider whether God was asking me to trust Him on my own account, apart from work at Wayside. That thought quite alarmed me. How I needed God's guidance!

It was at this point that I received a letter from a young girl who had come to Kent from Wales at the age of 18 to work with us at Kirkman (the name of the nursing home). She had left there soon after I did and I had heard she had married but had had no contact from her in years, until now. The letter told me that her marriage had failed miserably and she was now asking if she could come and stay for a week or two as she had 'not forgotten the Christian love and security she had experienced at Kirkman'. I remembered how concern and care for the staff at both of my previous jobs had been a challenge but also a real source of satisfaction. Such responsibility was not my remit at Wayside and I realised that I missed that. As I sat at my dining table in the window overlooking the garden, Denise's letter before me, I thought of a number of young people like her who had passed through my hands. 'More are the children of the desolate than the children of the married wife saith the Lord' were the words of Scripture that came to mind. Familiar though these words were, I could not have told you where in the Bible they would be found. Pulling my thoughts back to the present I realised that I would not at that point have felt up to entertaining someone 'for a week or two' and was glad to read that 'September or October' was what she had in mind.

During this time a church representative had been visiting in the absence of a pastor. An older man and a widower, I sometimes wondered whether his visits were more than pastoral in nature. I had no interest in such a relationship yet the thought of not having to work and being free to use my home to give such hospitality as my young friend was in need of was a very attractive proposition. But there was a mortgage to be paid and household bills to consider and I did not have a husband to support me. A voice which no-one in the room would have heard but which spoke clearly to my mind and heart said, 'Thy Maker is thy Husband'. 'Where did that come from?' I asked myself, somewhat startled. Again, these were familiar words but I could not have said where in Scripture they would be found.

Another such 'pastoral' visit occurred a few evenings later. I was left with the strong impression that I needed to seriously pray about this issue and was not a little troubled. It was a matter heavy on my heart and mind next morning. After hours of reading in bed I was reluctant to stir myself to get up. Although it was lunchtime I had little appetite, anyway. I had done my various readings for the day but simply to 'put off time' I decided I would read Spurgeon's daily devotional Cheque Book of the Bank of Faith, which was amongst the books beside my bed. The Scripture verse for that day was as follows: 'I will betroth thee unto me for ever; yea, I will betroth thee unto me in righteousness and in judgement and in loving-kindness and in mercies…'. I simply marvelled and praised God for settling my mind on the issue and enabling me to lay it down.

Wayside's period of testing had continued throughout the period of my sick leave which now ran into many weeks. Andy was exercised to know how long he should pay me when he could. I was equally concerned to know what God was saying to me about my future. It seemed as if He might be leading me towards trusting Him at a personal level for provision, but oh, how I needed to be sure! And how could He use these various strands of thoughts I had had to show me from His Word? I was beginning to feel ready for work again and the issue was urgent.

I arranged to go over to Wayside one Friday evening to talk to Andy and Claire and to share with them my thoughts thus far. When Friday evening came I felt quite unwell with a spike in temperature and the by now familiar muscle aches and pains, so the visit was postponed.

The following Sunday morning I awoke and remembered—for the first time ever – that it was the early morning time for the service of worship on Radio Scotland. I tuned in. To my utter surprise the service was coming from Stornoway Free Church of Scotland. A church well known to me although I had never been there at that time. I sat up in bed, my King James Authorised Version of the bible on my lap, knowing that that is the one that they would use. The reading was announced: Isaiah chapter 54. 'Sing, oh barren one, thou who didst not bear, rejoice, break forth into singing thou that hast not been in travail, for more are the children of the desolate than the children of the married wife saith the Lord… enlarge the place of thy tent…lengthen thy cords, strengthen thy stakes… Fear not for thou shalt not be ashamed: neither be confounded for thou shalt not be put to shame… for thy Maker is thy Husband…'. (From Isaiah chapter 54 vv.1-4).

I wept, and wept again as they sang the words of the Scottish metrical version of Psalm 73 vv. 24 and 26: 'Thou, with thy counsel, while I live wilt me conduct and guide…my flesh and heart doth faint and fail but God doth fail me never…'. Only God could have brought my seemingly random thoughts together in one place in Scripture like that! I was in no doubt that He was confirming His will for me. My Bible in my hands, the tears streamed down my face as I spoke to God the words in my heart: 'Mortgage or no mortgage?' 'Mortgage or no mortgage' was the reply. 'But whatever will people say?' By this time the Scripture reader had reached the end of the chapter and was reading the closing verses: 'No weapon that is formed against thee shall prosper and every tongue that rises against thee in judgement thou shalt condemn'.

God had spoken. Through tears of wonder and apprehension, I bowed my head and worshipped...

It was August 18th, 1985.

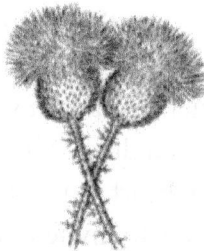

Chapter 16

Dusty

It was at this point that God did something particularly wonderful, confirming His personal interest in and love for me. Earlier chapters of this book have told of my affection for cats. Wherever I had been in life a cat – or cats – had been there too. Since coming to Bangor I had satisfied myself with a particularly cute poster of a kitten which someone had given me and I had it hung on my bedroom wall. Working long days, I had decided, would not be fair on a pet – even a cat.

I had seen a cat once or twice preening itself on top of the coal bunker outside my kitchen window and had learned that it was a stray which was being fed by various neighbours, but each household had a reason for not offering it a home. On the Saturday which began a week off, it was in my porch sheltering from the drizzling rain but scuttled off on my arrival. Next day, Sunday, I arrived home from church to find it there again. Just at that time there was much disharmony and unhappiness in the church fellowship I was attending. I had come home from worshipping with a heavy heart. I think the cat was as glad that day to be invited in as I was to invite him! I discovered that he was one of those cats that drool when happy. I can see us now— me with coat still on, cat on lap, his drool mingling with my dripping tears…

Andy and Claire's little girls at Wayside were very excited about Auntie Wilma's new pet. 'What are you going to call him?' was their cry. I replied that I had no idea – they would have to think of a name for him. I was duly presented with a list of names they deemed suitable for a cat, one of them being Dusty. Dusty it would be I told them, as he was indeed dusty having been 'sleeping rough' and uncared for. His white fur had become more of a shade of grey which resulted in a rather unkempt appearance. The provision of a home and regular food motivated him to take an interest in himself, though, and it was not long before his coat was clean, sleek and shiny, the white patches a sharp contrast with the black. He had a jagged white mark across one eye. I often told him that what he lacked in good looks he certainly made up for in character! He became quite 'kittenish' and I had to protect my velvet curtains! The vet who checked him over for me and pronounced him in good health reckoned he was under a year old. In fact there is good reason to believe that Dusty was in fact the young adult version of the little kitten that had got trapped in my porch several months earlier. Once found and released he had fled off into the night.

Dusty was wonderful company the weeks I was forced to spend in bed. It goes without saying that he was very happy to join me there! And it made me very happy when eventually he didn't feel the need to dash for cover whenever he heard the noise of the 'bin lorry' on its weekly round, he knew he was now safe. How many of his nine lives had he already lost, I wondered?

Thankfully he had at least one left to live with me and it turned out to be fifteen happy years long.

I had persuaded myself that I could never have a cat because of my long working days, but Dusty appeared on the final day of the very last fifteen day stretch of work at Wayside, no more long days! (Well, that's not quite true, I did frequently work very long days in the years to come, but mostly I came home at mealtimes.) And this little cat was already known to the neighbours and one of them was always willing to look after him when I needed to be away from home. No-one would ever be able to persuade me that God hadn't provided me with the comfort of that little animal – a wonderful affirmation of His love and care for me.

There was another evidence of God's amazing timing and provision. I had ordered a new telephone, one that would time my phone calls and help me keep costs down. It would be years yet before the invention of mobile phones. I had taken advantage of the opportunity to have a phone socket fitted upstairs beside my bed 'in case I should ever be unwell', and the work had been done the week before the need arose…

Chapter 17

Sharing the News

Now began the rather daunting task of sharing the news of what God had been saying to me over recent weeks. Andy and Claire at Wayside must be first to hear. On the Friday evening when I was prevented from keeping my arrangement of meeting with them, I had wondered if God were over-ruling, indeed He had over-ruled as on the following Sunday morning He had amazingly shown me so much more and now I had so much more to share! After listening attentively to all I had to say, Andy's immediate response was 'Well, that is how God leads me' and added that he could see and believe that God had been leading me and had indeed spoken through His Word. 'There's no arguing with God!' were his words. They understood that it would mean my leaving Wayside. They knew that I was praying very much about my future so they were prepared for such an event. We prayed together.

Andy requested that I personally give an account of God's leading to Mrs Ravey and Dorothy (Claire's mum and sister), who were the other members of the team. 'Because', said Claire, 'Mum knew you were struggling and may see this as a cop-out'. I knew only too well that there would be those who would not understand and think the same. I found myself trembling as I re-told my story to them and, on a later occasion, to my close friends Hadden and Betty Wilson. I was so afraid that they would not understand. Both Mrs Ravey and Hadden used the very same words when I had finished sharing: 'That has taken a lot out of you' – and it had! I was totally drained and exhausted. Most encouragingly, though, Hadden had added matter-of-factly: 'So God has made your next step plain. Let us thank Him'. And so we prayed and did just that.

At that time I was in the habit of communicating with two very close friends back in Scotland, Olive and Janet, and another, Kathleen, in Tunbridge Wells, by letter tape. So I dictated the now-familiar story on to tape and copied it for these three friends. Excited responses came from Olive and Janet by return of post. Not so from Kathleen, though. She wrote to Claire expressing her concern for me, adding: 'I find it difficult to distinguish between holy boldness and spiritual pride'. Jenny, the instrument God had used to bring me to Northern Ireland in the first place, was equally fearful and unbelieving and expressed her thoughts in no uncertain terms.

It was no surprise that our archenemy, Satan, would be busy with the most-used weapon in his armoury – discouragement. Had I really heard God aright? I found myself waking at an early hour and feeling that knot in the pit of my stomach – 'What had I done?' 'How could I possibly do this?' Unbidden came the familiar words of Scripture 'I cannot go beyond the word of the Lord to do less or more' accompanied by 'peace that passes understanding' and an immediate return to sleep. In the morning I hastened to find these words in Scripture. I thought I should find them in the story of Balaam in the book of Numbers.

On first skipping through that story I read in chapter 24 of Balaam saying to the messengers of Balak that he could not go beyond the word of the Lord to do either good or bad. Had I got it wrong? That disturbed me. I read the whole story thoroughly from the beginning. There in chapter 22 verse 18, I read of Balaam saying to the servants of Balak: 'Though Balak were to give me his house full of silver and gold, I could not go beyond the command of the Lord to do less or more'. I was comforted that it was God's Word that I had heard and much encouraged.

It was imperative that the elders of the Church be told and a meeting was arranged with two of them and the pastor. I requested the pastor's wife to be present for female moral support. As I proceeded to tell my story I was met with expressions of blank incomprehension. The emotional pressure was too great and I broke down in tears. When I got home the sense of not being understood overwhelmed me. I got ready for bed but could only pace the floor of my bedroom. At length, when I could formulate a prayer, I cried to the Lord saying that if I had a good earthly husband he would comfort me. 'You have said that you are my Husband, please would you not do that?' He did. Peace descended and I was able to climb into bed and lie quietly until eventually sleep overtook me. Once again my heart overflowed in love and thankfulness to Him for proving His reality to me and thus encouraging me to hold on in faith to the words He had spoken to me.

On the morning of December 15th our pastor announced that the following Wednesday evening's meeting would take the form of praise and testimony, giving opportunity for anyone to praise God for what He had done throughout the year. Immediately I knew I must speak up and not put off any longer. My heart beat so hard and loudly I felt everyone around me could hear! I was not without experience in giving testimony but this time was different. Every time I sat down to prepare the pen in my hand shook so much I couldn't write! I asked close friends to pray. 'Do you have to do this?', one asked. Yes, I was convinced I must.

On the Wednesday morning I was awake from 3 am but was much calmer. Up early, I shopped in Bangor market at 8 am. It was the day planned for taking Jenny, now wheel-chair dependent, to do her Christmas shopping. It was always a full day out, having lunch in town. My heart was strangely at peace, even Jenny's continued negativity ('I feel I should get a job myself to keep you'), was unable to undo it. From the start of the meeting in the evening I found myself simply wanting to praise the Lord. As I spoke the person directly in front of me averted her eyes every time they met mine – even that was not allowed to distract me. At the end of that meeting I saw in that person's face as she rose to leave, the look that must originally have given rise to the expression 'black with rage', something I had never seen before. That person went on in the days following to influence others. But I could not dismiss the fact that God had done a new thing for me that day so I thanked Him and took courage…

The next day I wrote in my journal: *'Someone for whom I have always had a great respect and with whom I have always had a warm relationship has been quite 'off' since I spoke last night. Others quiet, saying nothing. The devil says: "What if God does not meet your need and you have stood up there and made a fool of yourself and brought dishonour on the Lord?". My daily reading took me to Jeremiah chapter 1 this morning and in verse 17 I read "Do not be dismayed by them lest I dismay you before them". That challenged me and set me on my feet!'* A few days later I celebrated a happy Christmas Day when the guest I had to stay helped me take our meal to share with wheelchair-bound Sadie where we enjoyed each other's company and fellowship. This was now becoming a regular annual event. Sadie used to say that it was the one day in the year when she had company *all* day!

The year 1985 had come to an end. It had been a year of such significance. Only God knew what lay ahead, but whatever the new year was to bring, I was determined to trust Him.

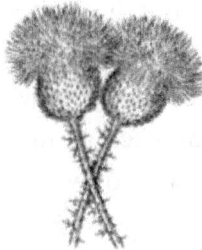

Chapter 18

Jenny

I introduced Jenny in chapter 10. Under God, Jenny was the instrument He used to point me in the direction of Wayside, or rather, the one God used to point Andy at Wayside in my direction. Jenny's MS meant that she was now wheelchair dependent. She lived with her elderly widowed father, now in his eighties, who was very disinclined to accept much-needed help from a stranger. I visited as a friend and he did not object when one day I got to work with the vacuum cleaner. As their need increased, so did my time with them. A later journal entry reads: '*I am now officially employed by Social Services for two hours on a Thursday as their Home Help. Jenny was not happy about my working for nothing and I was not happy about their paying me. This leaves us both comfortable!*'

Very soon the time I spent with them – voluntarily – increased until eventually I was going three days a week, doing the housework, washing and cooking. I remember the time spent persuading them both about the merits of a microwave oven. When eventually one was bought and installed, meals became much easier for Jenny to manage when they were alone. In turn, I have Jenny to thank for teaching me to use a pressure cooker as one had been regularly used by her mother in that kitchen. I had always had a fear of the pressure cooker, but just as they gained confidence and benefitted from the microwave oven, so I gained confidence with the pressure cooker and used one with great success in my own kitchen for many years thereafter.

Just before Christmas 1988 Jenny's father was admitted to hospital for a blood transfusion and investigations. A diagnosis of stomach cancer was made and his condition deteriorated very quickly indeed. On Monday January 9th after doing the usual chores and having lunch I took Jenny to visit her father in the hospital. His condition was so low that I stayed with her until after 7 pm when her brother was expected after he finished work. They were both there with their father when he died at 8.30 pm.

If I'd known I was going to be so long in the hospital I would never have left my car where I had parked it near the old front entrance of the Royal Victoria Hospital – a place notorious for car damage and theft. I found the back window broken open and the bag of Jenny's wet washing stolen – neither Jenny nor I had a washing machine at that time and I had been taking it home to hang on the line. An old pair of walking shoes had also 'gone walking' and, in addition, (to my great disappointment), a very good car torch which had been a Christmas present from the guests at Orcombeleigh.

I gave thanks that it was a clear frosty evening and I could drive the car home in spite of having an empty space where the back window should have been! I needed to get home as it was the evening of the monthly Slavic Gospel Association prayer meeting in my house and that evening we were expecting the local Mission representative to be with us to give his report.

The news that morning had told of the tragic British Midland plane which had crashed the previous evening near the runway of the East Midlands airport on its flight from London to Belfast International airport. More than forty people died. On hearing the news Marlene and I had agreed that out of that number from the tiny Province of Northern Ireland we were sure to learn of 'someone who knew someone'.

At the end of that chilly drive home from the hospital in Belfast, my house already filled with friends ready to listen and to pray, I found Marlene in the kitchen where she was busily preparing supper for everyone. There had been a phone call telling that a close friend of mine and her schoolboy son had been on that fateful flight and both were dead…I was obliged to go straight into leading our little prayer meeting.

A week later a mutual friend travelled from England for the funeral, courtesy of British Midland. They also provided a car on arrival – thus making provision for my transport to the funeral as my car was not yet fixed. Together we travelled to County Tyrone where the funeral attended by many hundreds brought some closure to a shocking event, though I grieved sorely for my friend with whom I had enjoyed precious fellowship.

In the meantime I had accompanied Jenny to her father's funeral and spent time with her in the now forlornly empty family home afterwards. It transpired in the weeks following that being over seventy, her father had been entitled to the services of a Home Help but that now the situation had changed. A Social Worker visited one day while I was working in their house. As I was showing her out she said to me that Jenny would now be employing and paying me privately.

Now I had been praying for some time about the fact that I was spending so much of my time with Jenny and her father that I was not finding the time needed to spend with others whom God had put across my path. While Dad was unhappy to have anyone he considered a stranger in the house to help, this need not be the case with Jenny herself. A local Home Help could do the everyday chores that I had been doing three days a week, while I would continue to be a friend for fellowship and trips out for shopping or just for pleasure. In any case, I would not be happy to be 'employed' by anyone and especially not a friend.

This was a hard conversation to have. Jenny found it difficult to understand my thinking and felt I was 'abandoning' her. Prayer was answered when she found herself getting on very happily with the pleasant woman engaged to help while I continued to be very much in her life on a social basis. The time came when I was particularly involved in helping with Jenny's removal from the family home to a convenient and comfortable apartment in a nearby sheltered housing development where she lived contentedly for several years, with support.

With her parents, Jenny enjoyed outings and holidays to Donegal and to the North Antrim coast. We shared an interest in the Africa Inland Mission. Their annual residential conference was held in the lovely Castle Erin Christian Conference Centre in Portrush on that magnificent coastline. It was a highlight for me as often as I could attend, and one year I was enabled to take Jenny with me. Together we thoroughly enjoyed the ministry and the fellowship with missionary friends we had both known for many years. Before returning home there was time for an outing. I have a photograph of Jenny, in her wheelchair, with the glorious backdrop of the strand at Portballintrae, a spot which held special memories for her.

Eventually hospital care was needed. Jenny's patience and quiet trust in God was evident to all throughout the twenty long years she spent there. I visited regularly – until the Covid pandemic struck in 2020 when two close family members were the only visitors allowed. Even as I was writing this in early 2022, God took Jenny home to the mansion He had prepared for her, ending our nearly sixty years of friendship here, but happily only until we can pick it up again there one day in the maybe-not-so-distant-future.

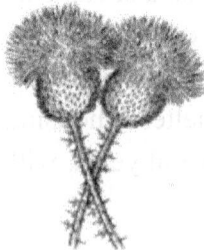

Chapter 19

Testing!

God has done amazing things for me down through the years
and has indeed shown me His glory in a variety of ways, not
least in leading and guiding me as I have made my way in life as
a lone individual. Now in this new phase of my journey
financial provision was going to be a crucial factor. It would be
in this way that I would prove the reality of His latest guidance.
Had I accurately interpreted His leading?

Wayside, as previously indicated, was being tested severely
during these months. While it was not possible for my wages to
be paid I had been marvelling at how God was continuing to
meet my needs. While I was praying about my future, Andy was
asking God how long he should pay me sick leave – when he
would be enabled to do so. Now that it was clear that I would
not be returning to work at Wayside Andy's prayer was no
longer relevant. As mentioned earlier he had often said: 'When
God wants to test any one of us He has to test us all.' And how
true this proved to be, because very soon after I discerned God's
will for me, which included my resignation from Wayside, gifts
were given to the work which enabled Andy to pay all wages
overdue as well as weekly wages as due from that point on. To
me it was a seal on God's guidance and it comforted me no end.
The other members of the team were as willing on this occasion

as on others to acknowledge and accept God's providence and I very much appreciated that, too.

I was paid the sick pay due to me now that Andy had the provision to do so. On Tuesday evening, October 29th I wrote in my journal: *'On Saturday evening I did some book-keeping. As my capital stands it could see me through a few months without undue concern. That makes it easier for me... I find that I am £170 behind in my tithing. Then there was a point earlier in the year when I thought that, if I could, I'd like to repay Wayside for the weeks I was paid but didn't work. It would be around £800. Now, at this point, do I still feel so generous?'*

At church that Sunday morning the sermon was on Genesis chapter 14 and concerned our priorities, tithing etc. I was saying in my heart 'Lord, if you have something to say to me here I am just too sluggish to hear this morning, please forgive me...' Right at the end of his sermon the pastor dealt with Abram's refusal to take anything from the king of Sodom. 'I wonder what Sarah thought' he mused, adding 'A woman likes to feel secure. Did she think "Look at all we could have had?"' At that I was jolted upright, all sluggishness gone. 'But look at the lovely touch at the beginning of the next chapter!' the pastor went on, and concluded by reading the first verse of chapter 15: 'Fear not, Abram; I am your shield and your reward shall be very great.' As tears coursed down my cheeks I knew in that moment that God was speaking to me.

The following Tuesday morning took me in my reading to the book of Zechariah and chapter 11. Verse 12 read as follows: 'If it seems right to you give me my wages but if not, keep them… and they counted out my wages… Then the Lord said to me "Cast it into the treasury"'. *'The Lord knows, I will need courage'* are the words recorded in my journal, followed by *'By the time I have paid out all I owe in the next few days there will not be much left… is it like Gideon's three hundred, I wonder? Did I have too much for God to show me His power?'*

In the days that followed, when at times both purse and bank account were completely empty and I was forced to lean heavily on my Heavenly Husband to meet my need, I thanked God that it was so because when without fail the need was met I knew beyond doubt it was His doing. If I had not given the £800 to Wayside as directed I would not have had the same need to be so dependent on God and would not have had the joy of the assurance that I was in His will for me.

How I praised and thanked Him!

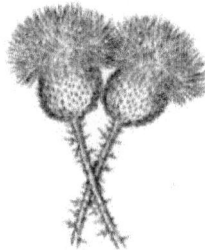

Chapter 20

And More Testing…

My journal's entry for March 28th, 1986, read as follows: '*I'm so aware that there is no earthly reason why anyone should support me, particularly when they cannot see what I am doing. The very nature of my work is confidential and I have adopted Wayside's principle that I tell no-one but God Himself of my need. Many ask, "Have you got a job yet?" I am continually saying to the Lord that He knows that I am in this position only because I believe He has brought me along this path. He knows that I am trusting Him not to have misled me and I am asking Him to vindicate His own Name before those who at this point are unbelieving. I am continually bringing before Him, too, His own Word "Fear not, you will not be put to shame…" My heart is amazingly at peace – truly it passes understanding.*'

Shortly after another journal entry reads: '*…at the moment I have not a penny towards the mortgage, not to mention rates and house insurance due next month etc. … the lack of anxiety I experience could only come from the Lord and day by day I get encouragement to trust Him in His Word. I know that in human terms it is crazy…*'

On Monday October 27th of that same year of 1986 my journal entry reads: '*Only a few days left of October. September and October mortgage payments not yet made. £100 remaining to pay on rates before the end of this month. This month is the end of my tax year and end of first full year of trusting God to meet my need. So much to praise Him for! He has been so wonderfully faithful. This morning in prayer I was impressed by the fact that my Husband handles all the bills in this house. Never before in my whole life have I known an earthly situation where I could trust anyone in this way. Even in childhood I carried the responsibility at home and ever since it has been up to myself. What a rest of heart! How I praise and love the Lord! "I'll praise Him for all that is past and trust Him for all that's to come." He has said: "Fear not, you shall not be put to shame."*'

A week passed. '*Saturday November 1st. No gifts except one £10 note, and that I have set aside as I was not happy because of the spirit in which it was given. I still have 'petty cash' because previous gifts still did not enable me to pay anything. Disturbed that the Lord does not feel as near as usual. Have been asking Him to reveal to me where I have gone wrong if that is the case, to forgive me and show me His mercy. I want to learn from this experience and avoid making the same mistake again. His word to me has not changed and I am hanging on to that*...

'*Monday November 5th. Nothing over the weekend or in this morning's post except notification of an increase in the mortgage interest rate!*

'*Saturday November 8th. Had a very precious time with the Lord this evening. Still no bills paid, but my Husband looks after the bills and He has said "Fear not…." Struck this evening by the meaning of "Perfect love casts out fear". Thank you, Lord, for returning your peace to my heart.*

'*Tuesday December 2nd. Small intermittent gifts only during November. Never quite enough to pay one month's mortgage although thankful to pay car account. Have been concerned that car due 10,000 mile service and it needs it – running 'rough'. Took it to garage today and paid the £52 bill as well as paying the telephone account, so back to square one! Stayed in today to spend time with the Lord. Reading took me to the later chapters of Ezra where he fasted and prayed for the sins of his fellow Jews. In spite of my concern for my duodenal ulcer I decided to fast, asking God to take care of my digestive system. Found it amazingly easy to do so as far as hunger was concerned. At tea-time I was preparing to bake a potato but was prompted to go back to Ezra, where I read (chapter 10 verse 6) that he "withdrew from the house of the Lord and went to the chamber of Jehohanan the son of Eliashib where he spent the night neither eating bread nor drinking water." Putting the potato back in the vegetable rack, I spent the rest of the evening in fasting and prayer. At bedtime I asked God to help me sleep* *in spite of having an empty stomach, and I did. How I praised and thanked God for being* <u>*real*</u> *with me! And next morning I awoke feeling really well and with more energy than usual.*

'Wednesday December 3rd. After paying bills yesterday I had to say that I would place usual order for coal today only if the post should bring £10 before the coalman came. It brought £20! However – also in the post was a reminder for the £100 due for the rates, and it must be paid within 7 days! I am amazed at the timing. That amount was due at the end of October, yet it comes the day after the Lord has assured me of His presence with me… I did not have long to pray this morning so took time at lunchtime to "spread the letter before the Lord." I asked myself what Scripture I should read before praying, I had read my OT, NT and Spurgeon in the morning. I picked up my little copy of Daily Light for the Daily Path which I hadn't used for months. I read their Scripture portions for that day. "I would seek unto God, unto God would I commit my cause" – Is anything too hard for the Lord? – Hezekiah received the letter…and went…and spread it before the Lord – it shall come to pass that before they call I will answer and while they are yet speaking I will hear. I love the Lord because He has heard the voice of my supplications. Because He has inclined His ear unto me I will call upon Him as long as I live." And how I say "Amen" to that last sentence! He took the burden to beseech Him to hear and answer my prayer away. I believed He had heard and I can only praise Him and trust Him… It might be thought that if only I hadn't had the car serviced yesterday and paid the telephone

bill I would have had enough today to meet this demand. But my heart is not chiding me. I believe the Lord is in all this and He will be the more glorified... He has said "You will not be put to shame..." I am always aware that BT doesn't wait long before cutting off the phone if the bill is not paid – praise Him He has never allowed me to be put to shame in that way.

'Thursday December 4ᵗʰ. For the first time ever, a gentle letter from the mortgage lenders reminding me how much I owe them. I marvel at the timing and continue to trust the Lord...The finance company to whom I pay the car instalments send a reminder smartly – it has happened 2 or 3 times – but the money has always been there as soon as the reminder. For months Bill has been saying that one day he'd come and have a look at the 'wee scrape' on my car. He phoned this morning and is coming on Tuesday! I am so thankful that the car has been serviced and is running well and I can answer all his questions honestly! I have not been put to shame...

Sunday 7ᵗʰ December. Was given an envelope before the evening service. It was quite thin and light. I found myself wondering if, for example, it contained £20 – could I make up the balance with what I had – was it £20 in my purse? And was it £10 or £20 in the bank? When I got home and opened the envelope it contained 3 X £50 notes!! My reaction was that I was standing on holy ground and that I myself was so wickedly lacking in faith and so easily taken in by the devil, succumbing to his wiles. How undeserving I am of the Lord's great love and faithfulness! How much I am learning of Him in these days! I can appreciate something of what Peter meant when he said: "Depart from me for I am a sinful man, O Lord!"

'Monday December 8th. The seventh day of the days given to pay the rates – and they were paid this morning.'

I could only smile and say nothing when an ex-pastor's wife on a return visit sardonically commented: 'I hear you have retired'. In fact as God opened up a wide variety of opportunities of service I found myself working hours which those in employment would describe as well beyond 'full time', while giving me job satisfaction well beyond anything I had previously experienced – and that for seventeen years!

But I'm leaping ahead...

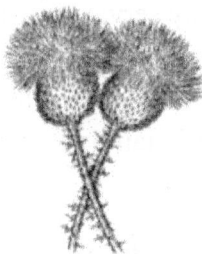

Chapter 21

The Mountain Goat

From 1972 until the nineties I drove a little Renault 4, commonly known as the Mountain Goat. Sadly Renault have not been making it for years now. The mountain goat and I have had many an adventure. I'll share one or two, beginning with one that goes back to the seventies when I worked in the Nursing Home in Kent.

I had been recommended the use of a certain garage to look after my car. The owner of the garage, which was quite a small one, always gave me his personal attention and regularly embarrassed me by calling me 'Matron' in front of other customers. Sporting sideburns, he was a dapper little man in a white coat such as doctors used to wear.

On presenting my car on one occasion I explained that I was going to be driving to the north of Scotland so the car needed to be dependable. It was duly serviced. The time to make the journey arrived. I reached Glasgow in rush hour in a horrendous thunderstorm and torrential rain. I still marvel and thank God that I reached my brother's family home on the west side of the city safely.

Well rested, I was ready for the road again next morning. I always took the route west up Loch Lomondside and across Rannoch Moor to Fortwilliam before swinging north up by Loch

Ness and on into Sutherlandshire. It was February and my brother was encouraging me to take the optional route which he considered the safer in winter weather but would have meant crossing the city from west to east – something I was not keen to do. In the end he said: 'Well, if you have confidence in your car…' I did have confidence in my car I assured him – after all it was newly serviced and checked! And so I set out.

Little cars like mine, in those days, did not have a built-in stereo system. I had hand-printed pieces of paper to fix on my dashboard with the words of familiar and well-loved hymns to sing along to while I drove.

Those familiar with that part of the world will know that Rannoch Moor is extensive and bleak and one would not expect to see much traffic on it in the wintertime of nearly fifty years ago. I remember it was drizzling and misty but I was happily driving along singing: 'The Lord is King, who then shall dare resist His will, distrust His care or murmur at His wise decrees or doubt His royal promises?'. (Josiah Condor 1789-1855) Just then a loud clattering interrupted my song and the car shuddered to a halt. Given the words I had just been singing I could only conclude that God was totally in control. I thanked Him that I was on a straight bit of road with no other vehicle close behind.

In the distance ahead a huge lorry was approaching. I got out of my car and indicated that I was in need of help. The very pleasant young lorry driver had a full tool kit in his cab and had me back on the road in no time although not before advising me that I should have the engine further checked at an early opportunity. Any reader in today's world will be conscious – as I was myself even then – of how vulnerable I was as a young woman alone on that lonely moor. But my Heavenly Father was with me and took perfect care of me and the situation. I reached my destination safely several hours later.

At that time my sister and family were living an hour's drive further north still, close to John o' Groats. Steep climbs and hairpin bends and another lonely moor lay between me and them. I came back from visiting very late one evening wonderfully safely but when I went to go out next day the car would not start! I had to call out the local mechanic, an experienced man I had known since childhood. He fixed me up for that day but said I would need to bring the car to him before driving back to the south of England. I did that, of course, and a sizeable bill followed…

When I got back to Tunbridge Wells I went along to my little garage man and showed him the bill. I assured him of my appreciation of his personal service but that I needed to have confidence in the work done. A few 'hmmm's' were murmured as he stroked his chin while taking in the details of the work that had been done in Scotland. "If I refund the amount of this bill, ma'am, will that make it all right?" Of course it did.

The following year the time came for me to leave Kent for Northern Ireland and I once again needed my car made roadworthy for the journey. I told the dear man where I was going and that I was going to be looking after disabled young people. Of course in 1981 'the troubles' were still ongoing. 'What do you want to do that for, ma'am? With the work that you are doing you are going to heaven already!' I was at pains to explain that my getting to heaven did not depend on the work I did. 'But it must do ma'am, it must do'.

Sad to say I didn't ever see him again to say goodbye. He did not come as usual to speak to me when I went to pick the car up that day. I had taken a thank you note and a small gift. I was told that the invoice wasn't ready for collection – it usually was. In spite of subsequent enquiries and leaving my new address I did not ever get that bill. I prayed then and do again now as I write that my explanation of Jesus being the only way to get to heaven might have lodged in his heart to his eventual salvation.

Many years later, on the afternoon of Christmas Eve 1984 to be exact, I arranged to pick up a friend with her shopping outside the supermarket that was then on Main Street in Bangor. A mother of four children, she would have had a lot of shopping. On my way, at an extremely busy junction, the mountain goat expired, it's clutch had given out! I have no memory of how I got in touch with my friend – did she get tired of waiting and get a taxi, I wonder? Still no mobile phones! Needless to say I felt dreadful for letting her down.

Andy lent me the Renault 4 which was one of the two cars that made up the 'fleet' used for the work at Wayside, allowing me to fulfil my plans for Christmas Day and Boxing Day which were to bring company and a Christmas meal to two different homes where there was disability. That car was returned on the 27th. For the rest of the holiday period I was 'grounded' – just the rest God knew I craved and needed.

On January 2nd, 1985, a new clutch was fitted to my car and I was greatly encouraged when the garage informed me that there were no other major issues outstanding, so when it was time for the annual MOT a few weeks later I presented it with more confidence than was often the case. At this point the car was thirteen years old and the MOT an annual major prayer point!

My confidence had been misplaced. This time several issues were raised, including issues with the bodywork. The garage's verdict was that the age of the car meant it was not worth the expenditure required, while giving me a quotation for the work that would be involved. What should I do? I was in no position to change my car. I remembered that I had been invited to friends for my meal the next evening and two men would be there who would be able to give me advice. As soon as the thought entered my mind my conscience rebuked me. Had I not covenanted before God not to let anyone but Him know of my need? I could say nothing about it when in their company next evening.

Next morning my daily reading took me to Psalm 31. 'In you, O LORD, I have taken refuge; let me never be put to shame; deliver me in your righteousness. Turn your ear to me, come quickly to my rescue; be my rock of refuge, a strong fortress to save me. Since you are my rock and my fortress, for the sake of your name lead me and guide me' (Psalm 31 verses 1-3 New International Version). 'For the sake of your name' were the words I plead in prayer as I cried to the Lord for His wisdom, guidance and help in my extremity and my heart was again given that peace 'that passes understanding'.

That evening, as always in that hospitable home, a thoroughly enjoyable meal was served before we all adjourned to the other room for an evening of comfortable conversation. Almost immediately the question was asked by one of the men: 'Wilma, when does your car go for MOT?' I had been put on the spot! I had no option but be truthful and say that it had been there the day before. Of course they wanted to know how the car had fared and once again I was forced to be truthful, adding that I was praying about what the Lord would have me do. I did notice that the second man was unusually quiet but I was relieved that the subject was then dropped.

Next morning I was hurrying downstairs past the telephone in the hall when it rang. I was running late for an appointment – should I stop to answer it? I did, only to hear the voice at the other end say: 'Wilma, I hear your car didn't pass it's MOT yesterday.' Without waiting for a reply the man went on to add the astounding words: 'That little car of yours is not worth spending money on. Do nothing at all about it until I come and speak to you. Some of us in church have been putting money aside for when you would need it for a new car.' To say that I was taken aback would be a gross understatement and with a heart full of praise and thanks to God for hearing my cry for help as well as thanks for the love of these anonymous friends, I hurried on to keep my appointment.

When we met to talk at midday I learned that enquiry had been made of the local Renault dealer. They were doing a deal. On payment of 25% of the cost of a new Renault 4 (which cost the friends' gift would cover), there was 0% interest on the remainder, paid in monthly instalments. Later that day my good friend – an astute business man – accompanied me to the garage where the appropriate documentation was drawn up.

My existing MOT certificate allowed me to continue driving my old car until March 6th. On March 7th my new car was ready for collection… Who but the Lord could do it? He had kept His word and my heart sang His praise.

A few weeks later I was asked to give testimony at church and this story was told. I ended with the verse 19 of that same Psalm 31: 'How great is your goodness which you have stored up for those who fear you, which you bestow in the sight of the sons of men.' That new car sat outside the church in sight of all! And verse 21: 'Praise be to the LORD for he showed his love to me when I was in a besieged city.' All praise to Him indeed!

Little did I know just then, in the Spring of 1985, what the next weeks and months would hold – illness and a complete change of direction, one which would mean my looking to the Lord as an individual to meet all my needs including financial. But God, as ever, was faithful. My journal entry for Tuesday 29th September,1987, reads: '*A momentous month! I PAID THE LAST INSTALMENT ON THE CAR! I cannot praise the Lord enough. 30 payments of £104 – and only one or two of them while I was still in employment in Wayside. While I have no words to express the wonder I feel, yet it is only as God promised in Isaiah 54: "Fear not, you shall not be put to shame."* '

This new version of 'the mountain goat' became a familiar sight around Bangor – there were not so many of them in circulation by this time. In the following twelve years it clocked up many miles in the Lord's service as I was now using my car continually for work, something my previous one had not had to do. In fact the time came that, for me a day off meant one that the car didn't leave the driveway! Once again I had a car that was showing its age. This fact was brought forcibly to my attention by one of the young people I was transporting to a GCU (Girl Crusaders' Union), event in 1997. As we drove along her voice from the seat behind me was heard to say: 'No offence, Miss Nicolson, but this car of yours is dead old!' Onlookers even commented when they observed the rust on the bodywork. But how could I ever replace it?

A very kind and generous friend was changing her car and offered me her old one. I said I would consider accepting only on the condition that I would be enabled to give her the trade-in price that the garage was offering. Even that was far beyond my reach but the matter was taken to the Lord in prayer. At that time one and another Building Society was becoming a bank and their customers were given a share. God prompted one who said that she had had hers and did not need it at that stage in life. It was given to me. It was the exact figure that my friend had been offered by the car salesperson as the trade-in value of her car! That car served me well for the remaining eight years of my working life and into retirement, at which point I sold it 'for a song' and have felt no need of a car since.

Thirty-one years of driving. Safely kept. Many a flat tyre on both mountain goats – I never did discover why! There were mysterious noises from the engine, more than once just when a visitor was due to stay and expected to be driven around. And there were also 'breakdowns'. I never ceased to marvel at the evidence of God's care. On each and every occasion it was experienced either in the form of safety for myself and passenger if I had one, help readily on hand or finance to meet the need. God has been so consistently faithful. But then, did He not promise 'You will not be put to shame?' He was simply keeping His Word!

Chapter 22

Visitors

Denise's request to come and stay for 'a week or two' was happily fulfilled in the autumn of 1985. We are still in touch. She has been married to a faithful husband and has great joy in her four lovely grandchildren from her only son.

At a later stage another request was also honoured. Audrey was the widow of a lovely young policeman whom I had helped care for many years before in Orcombeleigh, the MS Holiday Home in Devon. I wrote then of how she had written telling me of John's death and asking that she might continue to be a friend 'for her own sake'. John's parents had lived with their son and his family, helping to care for him and their two children, allowing policewoman Audrey to continue working. Now John's mother had died, the last of her generation, and Audrey was very bereft. 'Why do I find old age so sad?' She asked if she could come to visit.

I met Audrey at the airport on Monday afternoon. I would not have recognised her, but she recognised me. It had been more than ten years since we'd met. I had prayed much as I didn't know her and did not know what to expect. She had obviously come just to *talk*. Although we went out sight-seeing on Tuesday and Wednesday she did not see anything, she just talked. 'I've talked about things I've been needing to talk about for a long time.' By Thursday she had 'talked herself out' (her words). That day was May Day and God blessed us with a glorious day for driving around the North Antrim coast and Audrey appreciated it in all its splendour. I did the talking as we drove home, and shared much of what Jesus meant to me and what He had done in my life. 'Listening to you is like listening to a talking book! If I didn't know you I would think it was all fable.' Parting at the airport on Friday my guest's parting words were 'I'm so glad I came!' and my heart praised and thanked the Lord.

Many others, with a variety of needs, visited or stayed as the occasion demanded. Sometimes their stay was longer than planned. Such was the case on one of the number of holidays June spent with me. June was a former work colleague who had been left by her husband to bring up her three children alone. The children now left home; June loved to come. Over the years she showed considerable interest in the Christian faith, only God knows whether she ever truly trusted Him before her death a few years ago now, but many were the profitable conversations between us.

June came at Easter one year. On Easter Saturday we took an outing to the North Antrim coast and walked the coastal path from Runkerry towards the Giant's Causeway. The weather had been very wet. June slipped on a muddy stretch of path and broke her leg. Walkers on their way to the Causeway raised the alarm. Eventually paramedics arrived and took the decision that an airlift was necessary. Poor June! Thankfully it wasn't raining but it was not a particularly warm April day. It was a long wait of several hours lying on the hard stony ground at the edge of the path above the sea and a stay in Northern Ireland of four weeks rather than the one planned! The news item on Radio Ulster telling of the 'elderly lady' who had to be airlifted to hospital didn't go down too well either, since June was just in her early sixties at that time!

Some things couldn't be achieved in my wee home in Bangor. It needed a much larger house to enable the four elderly folk plus myself and a helper to attend the Portstewart Convention – or Keswick at Portstewart as it is now known. Each of these folk had precious memories of attending the Convention over the years, for some accompanied by their life's partner. It gave great pleasure to enable them to relive some of these memories. These were great times of enjoying the meetings, afternoon outings and fellowship with each other around the meal table. It was something that was repeated each July for several years.

Mary and Arthur from East Sussex also visited soon after my arrival in Northern Ireland. On the evening of their very first day we sat looking out over Strangford Loch to watch the sunset. The tide was out. The murmuration of a flock of small seabirds seen against the red sunset sky was unforgettable. So, too, was the sight and sound of the white-topped crashing waves on a sunny, windy day at the Giant's Causeway. By contrast, a seat in the sun watching the reflection of the surrounding Mountains of Mourne in the still waters of the reservoir in the Silent Valley was a benediction. They loved it all and I so enjoyed their company and fellowship. Already gone ahead of me to heaven, I look forward to renewing fellowship with them both one day.

A special visitor was my long-standing friend from student days, Elizabeth Mantell. Known to many in both Scotland and Northern Ireland through her missionary work with the Presbyterian Church in Malawi, there were a number of others she visited each time she came – fellow missionaries who had worked with her in Africa. Readers have met Elizabeth earlier in this book as it was she with whom I was holidaying in 1981 when God confirmed to me the rightness of my relocating to Ulster. So sadly, cancer took dear Elizabeth from us while still in her fifties – another with whom I look forward to being reunited one day.

On a happier note, it was a great occasion when I entertained about thirteen family members in my garden on a hot summer day in the nineties! They were here for a nephew's wedding the next day. Some of them had been very apprehensive about coming to our troubled Province, but in the event a very good and safe time was had by all.

All praise to God for family and friends and for His blessing, safe-keeping, provision and enabling.

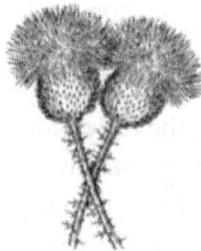

Chapter 23

Refurbishing Fever

In the summer of 1988 one of my easy chairs collapsed irreparably as one of the wooden legs broke. It was part of a little three-piece suite I had bought from the 'Small-Ads' in the weekly Spectator when I had bought the house. This particular chair had been in use in the little dining-room at the back of the house where I sat during the summer months as the room was south-facing and caught the sun all day. That summer, in the absence of the chair, I used a folding garden lounger in the dining-room.

In August I was expecting two visitors to stay for the weekend of the annual Missionary Convention (now known as Bangor Worldwide). One of the speakers expected that year was Georgi Vins, the Russian pastor previously imprisoned by the Soviet authorities for his involvement in a network of Baptist Churches and a man whom we had prayed much for over the years. His daughter Natasha was to accompany him and when the time came several friends and myself were privileged and thrilled to fellowship with Natasha over a meal in a friend's home.

I did want to replace my chair before my visitors would arrive at the end of the month so I scoured the 'Small-Ads' again as well as local second-hand shops, all to no avail. While maintaining my practice of not sharing with anyone but the Lord my current need, I heard one day while visiting someone that a certain missionary couple I knew were retiring. Having been allocated a council flat they were to set up home for the first time in this country. Someone from church had got in touch to say that since their mother had died they were welcome to visit her bungalow and choose whatever they wanted to furnish their flat and the items would be delivered. I praised God for meeting their need and thanked Him for reminding me of what God was able to do. I determined there and then to trust Him to meet my need in His time while accepting that I would have to entertain my friends without that dining-room chair.

On Saturday August 20th a phone call began: 'A friend's mother has gone to live with her daughter. The little suite from her front room is in his garage. I don't suppose you would be interested, would you?' Would I! The caller went on: 'Of course the colour may not suit or you may not like it at all, you'd have to see it.' I knew that it was so obviously God's provision that I would not be arguing with Him! On Monday 22nd I called to see the suite. The colour was perfect, but it *was* small, smaller than I had already, but it was the Lord's provision and I accepted it gratefully – as well as a little unit which was exactly what I had been looking for to fill the alcove by the fireplace.

On Saturday 27th, just hours before my visitors arrived, the articles were brought to my home. I found that because the chairs were smaller I could have two comfortably in the dining-room and this three-seater settee matched acceptably the existing two-seater settee in the living-room so I now had more seating than before. *Of course* God knew best and I was thrilled with His provision.

Another, much greater, need was for replacement windows and front door. The wooden frames around the single-glazed windows were rotting and the door flimsy. How could I ever see such a major job done? It was made a matter of prayer.

One amazing day a letter came from an unknown solicitor in Scotland. A far-out cousin of my late father's, someone I had had no knowledge of, had died intestate and my brother, sister and I were to share my father's inheritance. My share was exactly the amount required to replace my windows and door.

The tiny kitchen in number 75 badly needed upgrading. It was now well over ten years since I had moved in and nothing had ever been done there. A journal entry of the time reads as follows: *'From the Spring of the year I have been concerned that redecoration is overdue in the kitchen but much more than decorating needs to be done. There is so much room for improvement! The taps at the sink are uneven, plumbing is exposed. Plaster on the walls of the big old larder is crumbling. There is not enough room for two people to work together at the sink so that one can dry dishes. More cupboard space is needed... I have thought and prayed, spending hours wondering what I would do if I could. Gradually the best solution has*

131

formed in my mind and been talked through with Andy and another friend for advice.'

Wonderfully, the usually non-existent balance in my savings account began to grow sufficiently to convince me that God was with me in it and I should begin to look seriously at who I should ask to do the work. I couldn't ask any of the large kitchen firms to do my little job which would include fitting second-hand units. My own church had bought the property next door and it was being demolished. An 'as new' three-door kitchen wall unit was rescued before going to the skip! Also I had bought a cooker hood advertised in the local paper for £25.00.

I determined to be patient and wait for God to guide, which He did in His time. Marlene mentioned a tradesman in her church who had made units for Andy. When approached he came readily to see what was required and pronounced everything 'no problem'. An electrician friend from church was engaged to do the electrical work.

All this was happening just before I began a two-week stint of looking after an elderly lady in Belfast while her niece who lived with her got a break. The cheque the niece left for me, together with what was in my savings account, came exactly to the total amount required to meet the cost of the whole job. How I praised and thanked God! On completion of the work my journal records: *'The work was done on Saturdays, thus spreading it out over several weeks. However now it is all done (except for the decorating), and the result is most satisfying. I am thrilled with it and enjoy being in it. Removing the larder has let in more light and it all seems bigger and brighter... I could not have imagined ever having a kitchen like it is now. I am humbled and thankful and am praising God from a full heart.'*

I had not ever been able to afford a washing machine but would have had nowhere to put one anyway. In faith I allowed space when the kitchen was reconfigured. Shortly after the work was done, someone who knew nothing about that asked if I did not have a washing machine because I could not afford it or because I had no space for one. I could honestly say that I previously had no place to put one but now I did have! Her sister whom I had helped care for had died and she wanted to give me a washing machine as a token of appreciation...

In 1989 a newly married young couple moved in next door. Paul wanted to erect a wooden fence between our back gardens to provide privacy. I was very happy about this as the wire fence was sagging and the rough grass growing around the fence posts was impossible for me to eradicate and very unsightly. When the new fence was in place, I was taken by surprise when two retired men from church offered to 'landscape' that side of the garden for me. My journal records that these two men – affectionately dubbed 'Bill and Ben' – *'worked like trojans'*. When they were finished I had by the fence a border for flowers separated from a vegetable plot by a paved path. The corner at the top of the driveway had a patio rendered more private and sheltered by the building up of the wall with decorative openwork bricks and a wooden gate from the driveway meant I had a completely enclosed and private back garden. It was beyond anything I could ever have dreamed of having…

These are just some of the ways that over the years God showed His love for me, making financial and practical provision and enabling me to care for and upkeep the wonderful home which He had provided for me and where I lived so comfortably and contentedly for over twenty-one years.

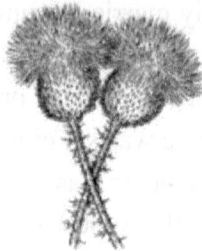

Chapter 24

GCU and Wind-Up

At the end of 1990 an appeal was made at church on behalf of a Christian girl, who needed lodgings in Bangor. I had a spare room – was this not a need that I could meet? The question was made a matter of prayer. The result of this enquiry was that Sarah, a young teacher in a nearby school came to share my home for four years until she bought one of her own. This led to my being introduced to Cherrie, a friend of hers who visited and became a friend of mine for life. In fact I am now happy to call her an 'honorary daughter' and her help and support in my older years is truly God's provision for me.

The coming of these two girls into my life opened up a completely new avenue of service for me. I was introduced for the first time to the Girl Crusaders' Union (GCU) and became a leader in that organisation, teaching Scripture to girls in the weekly Bangor class and taking girls to camp in different places all over the UK once or sometimes twice a year. Working irregular hours and many weekends as a nurse had prevented my involvement in youth work although I did teach Sunday School in my local church during the years I was unemployed while looking after the family in early life.

The years sped by very busily. God gave me a great variety of work to do. I certainly was glad of the experience I had had in caring for the elderly, but there was involvement at quite the other end of life, too. Just this week I had a visit from a friend who greeted me with the words: 'Thirty-three years ago today you had tea in my house!' Intrigued, I commended her on her good memory but asked for an explanation. It was her younger son's thirty-fourth birthday that day and seemingly I had been at his first birthday party! She had had a difficult pregnancy which required lots of rest and she had two pre-schoolers at home. I saw a lot of them all over a period of months and was the first after his father to see that new baby on the day he was born. He now has two children of his own.

Another young mum had her third child just as the first was about to start school. I did the school run each morning at first, while taking the younger sibling once a week to 'Tumble Tots'. I was available as a 'baby-sitter' to each of these families. On one occasion I stayed with three teenagers while their Mum spent two weeks in hospital after surgery.

Several friends, each with a physical disability, were enabled to have holidays over the years, with support. Sometimes it was the carer who needed a break, so having someone to step in to care made that possible.

At times I became very tired indeed and began to look longingly towards retirement. I realised, though, that such was the investment of time in certain people's lives and such was their dependence on me that I could not, and would not, have 'abandoned' them. Sometimes when a particular situation was occupying a great deal of my time I would think about how much I would miss that involvement when I was no longer needed, but that was never allowed to happen. There was always another need waiting in the wings and the work went on, seamlessly, that is, until my late fifties.

At that point what I have just described that there was always another need waiting in the wings, did not now always happen, causing me to ask God what He had in mind. I came to realise that many if not most of the situations I had been involved in had been years in duration. Now close to the age of retirement, to commit to another such involvement would not have been appropriate, I could not have seen it through. I marvelled to think that God had had all that in mind before I did!

Just at that time GCU had been given the financial resources to fund a representative to work in each area of the UK with the aim of expanding and consolidating the work. It would be a part-time post for a period of three years. Now with some time to spare and just three years to work until my sixtieth birthday, I applied for the Northern Ireland post and was appointed.

As with many part-time posts, this one often occupied nearer to full-time hours and along with my existing work made for an even busier life, but one that I enjoyed. The job involved some administrative work. Just at that point a cheque for £1,000 arrived in the post. It was from a friend from my days in Kent, a colleague long retired. 'Don't wonder at it, I must shed some' said the note that accompanied the cheque. It bought my first computer – a bulky desktop edition. Embarking on a course at the local Technical College I entered the digital world. Life with a mobile phone began at that time, too. How technology has advanced since then, much faster than my competence in using it!

My little car was now clocking up the miles travelling around the Province. How thankful I was for my new(er) more dependable model! A new GCU group in County Fermanagh was established. This meant a trip to the south west every other Saturday morning, picking up a fellow-leader in Lisburn on the way.

School visits promoting the work resulted in more girls enrolling as 'Lone Crusaders' and they were visited in their homes, some in County Londonderry. These girls completed attractive age-appropriate Bible studies which they sent to a 'Lone Leader' by post. I became a Lone Leader. Girls enrolled from aged nine. Two of these girls, now aged over thirty, were particularly diligent, forming a strong personal bond and I now thank God for the two 'honorary granddaughters' He has given me!

Thus ended the final seventeen-year span of my working life. While I had enjoyed each one of the different things God had given me to do, these final years were surely the most fulfilling, not least because of how I had proved my ever-faithful, gracious God. He, as no-one else, knew about the struggles, the temptations and yes, the failures at times during those years.

But in His faithfulness He had not let me be 'put to shame' as His word to me from Isaiah chapter 54 had promised.

Leading me to Northern Ireland in 1981 through my reading of Jeremiah chapter 31, verse 14 had particularly spoken to me and encouraged me at that time. An unknown future was before me. 'My people shall be satisfied with my goodness, says the Lord'. I believed for the fulfilment of that word from God. Now twenty-one years later I could say that that word had been abundantly fulfilled. I was totally satisfied with my God and His goodness to me.

Yes, goodness and mercy *had* followed me all the days of my life. I praised Him for all that was past and committed all that was to come to the same faithful God who is the same yesterday, today and forever!

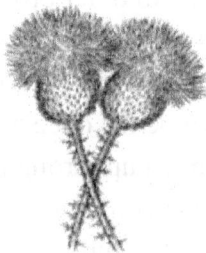

Postscript

The time had come to return to 'the home country'. I was eager to get there! Helmsdale, I believed, was too far north for ease of travel, either for myself or any who might want to visit. In a remarkable way God directed me to Arbroath in the county of Angus. While being on my beloved sea coast with beach and clifftop walks, Arbroath was remarkably conveniently placed with rail links to Glasgow, Edinburgh, Perth, Aberdeen and Inverness. And God answered prayer in finding me a home that was less than five minutes' walk from the train station.

During my time there I got involved in the local church, hosting a prayer group for Christians persecuted for their faith and taking part in an initiative partnering with local schools. A number of church members went regularly into school to help children with reading. I also helped a single mum by being available for her four primary-school aged children so that she had some time to herself. An older brother was usually out playing football with his mates. Over time, the youngest of the children in that family came regularly to me for tea and help with homework. This happened once a week at first, increasing to twice a week as he moved up through school. It was a great joy to finally hear him read confidently. Together we baked his birthday cake each year. One summer I took the three youngest to Bangor for a holiday to include the annual week-long children's Mission held at the seaside weather permitting – and it did that year! As a youngster Harris was fascinated with

140

aeroplanes. 'I've never seen a jet close up'. That flight to Northern Ireland was a first for them all and the whole holiday was a great success. As I have heard him say himself recently 'We had such fun!' Now in his twenties and a professional ballet dancer, I thank God for giving me in Harris an 'honorary grandson'.

I joined a walking group during my early years in Arbroath, thus making new friends and getting to know a part of Scotland previously unexplored – that is until I fell on the ice and broke my wrist and then went on to get my first-ever dog, a re-homed Cairn Terrier called Bobby!

Beautiful as the county of Angus is, it is not culturally Highland and I began to sense that the time was approaching – as I always knew it would – for me to think of relocating. From time to time I went north for special family occasions and had begun to feel it each time more of a wrench to journey south again. However the time was not yet quite right. Harris's mother was given a serious cancer diagnosis and the very elderly neighbour in the flat below me was needing considerable support. I would not abandon either of them.

A year later Harris's mum died and he moved away to live with an aunt. At that point, he was about to transfer from primary to secondary school. My elderly neighbour was now on the brink of moving to a place of care. Bobby, my much-loved elderly dog was ready to be 'put to sleep'. My flat was sold and I found a place to live in the village of Alness, twenty or so miles north of Inverness where my sister and husband lived and approximately seventy miles south of Helmsdale where my brother and his wife lived in our childhood family home.

Weeks after moving a cousin unexpectedly died. Within the next year my brother died of the cancer he had had for years followed six months later by my sister, only months after she had been given a cancer diagnosis. Fourteen months after my sister's death my brother-in-law also died. A few short months later we were shocked by the death of a nephew due to a fire in his flat in Edinburgh. It was a traumatic time, but so right that I should have been living amongst them. During that same first year I myself had surgery to remove a small malignant tumour followed by weeks of radiotherapy.

A few years of re-adjustment followed during which time I adopted another little Cairn Terrier, Cindy. Thrice-daily walks with her down by the river or up into the forest behind my house were therapeutic. Some chest pain meant a diagnosis of mild cardiac problems. Public transport in the area became more limited and transport to church each Sunday became more problematic.

I found myself rather isolated. I had maintained many friendships back in Bangor and a strong link with the church there, so after much prayer and heart-searching, it was to Bangor I was to return and make my home again, this time in supported housing, close to the town centre and very close to church. I had been back in Scotland for fourteen years.

Six years later and my eightieth birthday is behind me. It is in the very comfortable little apartment which I am persuaded God chose for me that I have written the foregoing. And all that has been written has had but one object in view, that God may be exalted, worshipped, praised and glorified. There is so much more that could have been said, so many more words written – but quoting John chapter 20 and verse 30: 'These are written that you may believe that Jesus is the Christ, the Son of God, and that believing you may have life in his name'.

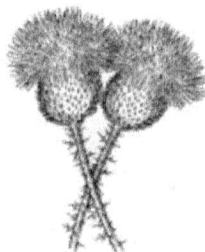